How to Know if Someone
Is Worth Pursuing in

two
dates
or less

How to Know if Someone
Is Worth Pursuing in

two
dates
or less

NEIL CLARK WARREN

THOMAS NELSON PUBLISHERS®
Nashville

Published in Nashville, Tennessee, by Thomas Nelson, Inc.

Library of Congress Cataloging-in-Publication Data

Warren, Neil Clark.
   How to know if someone is worth pursuing in two dates or
less / Neil Clark Warren
     p.   cm.
   ISBN 0-7852-6904-5 (pbk.)
   1. Mate selection. 2. Dating (Social customs) 3. Man-
woman relationships.   I. Title.
   HQ801.W2957 1999
   646.7'7—dc21   99-16843
                                                      CIP

Printed in the United States of America
4 5 6 7 QPV 05 04 03 02 01 00

This book is dedicated to
Gregory Thomas Forgatch
and Lorraine Warren Forgatch
who lovingly introduced me to the
critical importance of wise mate selection.

CONTENTS

ACKNOWLEDGMENTS

First, I want to acknowledge the help of my close friend and colleague Greg Forgatch. He is really the coauthor of this book, and without his thinking and encouragement, it never would have seen the light of day.

As usual, my friend and editor Keith Wall made a significant contribution to this project. This is our fifth collaboration, and it gets better every time.

Rolf Zettersten, publisher at Thomas Nelson, has learned the secret of giving freedom and transmitting positive reinforcement.

Absolutely nothing that I do would be possible without the faithful and competent help of my administrative assistant, Sue Braden.

And, of course, it would be impossible to do justice to my feelings of love and appreciation for my wife and companion, Marylyn Mann Warren. She is the one who has taught me virtually everything I know about loving and living.

INTRODUCTION

WHY YOU MAY WANT TO READ THIS BOOK . . . AND WHY I WANT YOU TO READ IT

Let me get right to the point. You may want to read this book because you're sick and tired of dating people for too long with nothing coming of it. Perhaps you keep discovering that the people you date are just not right for you—but you waste too much time figuring it out. The fact is that you could have known this before the end of two dates. The secret is to learn how to identify dead-end relationships quickly so you don't have to invest more time, energy, and caring than are necessary—and so you can move on to more promising possibilities.

Here is a second reason you may want to read this

book: Dating efficiency is a function of clear thinking; you become more and more "dating proficient" as you learn to think clearly about yourself and the person you want to marry. If you're fuzzy about the qualities you *must have* in a lifelong mate, or if you're unsure about the qualities you *can't stand*, your efficiency level is bound to be lower than you would like. This book deals directly with your "must-have" and "can't-stand" lists, and when you finish building these lists to your full satisfaction, you will have become a veritable expert on the art of dating.

And third, I promise that when you have read through this book—and implemented the strategies I recommend—you will be significantly more attractive to the person you most want to marry. If that's not reason enough to read this book, I don't know what is!

This is how it works. Once you get to know yourself well, and once you figure out exactly the kind of person you want to marry, you are much more likely to know this person when he or she comes along. You will be able to pick the person out of a crowd. And if there's anything better than that, it's being picked out of the crowd *by* the love of your life. When you get treated wonderfully by someone who thinks you're the very person they've been looking for, you are bound to find that person far more attractive than you ever found anyone before. The fact is, all of us are dying to feel good about ourselves, and when we feel especially good around a certain person, we will be amazed at how important and attractive that person becomes for us—and vice versa.

So here, in snapshot form, are the three reasons *you* may want to read this book:

1. You want to leave behind a miserable, time-consuming, going-nowhere dating process.

2. You want to know exactly what you are doing when you date, exactly the kind of person you want to marry, and exactly how to get the best results from the dating process.

3. You want to be maximally attractive to the very person who attracts you most.

AND HERE ARE THE REASONS *I* WANT YOU TO READ THIS BOOK . . .

First, wise dating would increase the percentage of successful marriages and, naturally, reduce the number of failures. A huge number of all marriage failures could be avoided if people were taught to deal with their relational difficulties early in the dating process. Why? Because too many couples continue going with each other long after it is obvious that their relationship has major defects. The longer they date, the harder it is to go their separate ways. A shockingly large number of couples never muster the courage to break up, and they end up getting married. These marriages are doomed from the beginning.

Second, I want you to read this book so you can be part of a revolution in the world. If it is true that failed marriages and family breakdown are significant causes of the social chaos, violence, and turmoil around the world (and there is overwhelming research to support this claim), then let's begin doing something about it. If you follow the principles for marrying the right person, you will be successful at the most important part of human living. Moreover, you will become so confident about your expertise that you will share it with your friends, family members, and anyone who will listen. If we can reduce the divorce rate in the United States by just 5 percent, this will affect more than one million people in a generation (not to mention the millions in the following generations). Even more exciting, if we can reduce the divorce rate in our country to single digits, it will represent the most important social revolution in the history of the world.

Is all this too lofty and far-fetched? I don't think so! I

want to be part of that change—along with you—and I can't think of anything more exhilarating than making a positive contribution to the millions of people who will get married in the coming years, along with their children and grandchildren. Won't you join me?

Chapter 1

WINNING AT THE DATING GAME

A distressed woman pulled me aside after a speaking engagement for singles.

"I'm Christy, and I need your help," she announced.

"What seems to be the problem?" I asked.

"I've been dating my boyfriend, Steve, for a year, but now I'm convinced we're not right for each other."

I asked how she'd come to that conclusion.

"Lately, all kinds of things have started coming up. Like, Steve is really bad at managing his money. Last month, he lost three hundred dollars betting on football, and then he had to borrow the money from me to cover his rent. Things like that are always happening."

"You're right—if that's a pattern, it could be trouble," I said. "Anything else?"

"Oh, all kinds of things. Steve loves to talk about himself, but he *never* asks about me—my job or friends or anything. It's like our relationship is totally focused on him. I need someone who shows at least a *little* interest in me."

"You say you've been dating for a year?" I asked. "Did you notice these things before?"

"I guess I wasn't really looking for them. But as time went on, I've seen how incompatible we are. And I have to admit, it seems like I've wasted a year when I could have been dating other people or pursuing other goals."

Christy's dilemma is a common one. I've talked with hundreds of single men and women who stick with dead-end relationships month after month even though it's clear the couple is ill-suited. By persisting with a relationship that's going nowhere, they waste valuable time, fan false expectations, and create unnecessary heartache and hurt.

The truth is, millions of American singles would love to get married—but only if they could live happily and forever with their partner. The vast majority of single men and women, however, are fed up with the dating game. The whole frustrating, exhilarating, maddening, crazy process leaves them feeling confused, baffled, and hopeless.

Are you one of them?

Does a happy marriage seem light-years away because of the impossible challenges of dating?

Have you found dating a painful, sometimes frightening, endlessly puzzling pursuit?

Would you like to cut down on the hassle, seriously reduce the confusion, and move efficiently and smoothly through the process?

Let me tell you how I think this book can help:

First, I'll help you analyze dating for exactly what it is. Sure, it's a frustrating, bewildering process for most people, but you can clear away all the haze and move into the dating arena with more self-assurance than ever before. We will look squarely at the three fundamental challenges of dating—and we'll simplify, clarify, and make it 100 percent more manageable. You'll learn to steer clear of all the quagmires and traps. You will encounter easy-to-apply guidelines that will move you like a rocket toward that person with whom you can be happy for the rest of your life.

Second, we'll get down to the nitty-gritty, practical aspects of dating. I'll show you exactly how to take charge of the critical, early phases of a relationship—how to make a quick and accurate decision about whether or not to invest more time, effort, and energy in another person. This will bolster your confidence and maximize your ability to handle every challenge dating brings.

For instance, if a member of the opposite sex asks you

out, you will know early on if he or she is "in the ball-park" for what you want in a lifetime companion. By the end of the second date, you will know precisely if you want to devote additional time and emotion to this person.

If you don't want to, you will have the confidence to end the relationship kindly and efficiently, treating the individual with dignity, but getting on with your effort to find the "right" person. If you conclude, somewhere between the first five minutes of the first encounter and the end of the second date, that this person has real promise for you, your decision will be bold and obvious . . . because it will be built on time-proven principles and a carefully honed methodology.

How Do You Know If Someone Is "Right" for You?

It is absolutely critical that you get your thinking straight about the type of person you want to marry. Sometimes singles fail to think strategically about potential mates simply because they don't have a wide range of candidates to choose from. They don't believe they'll ever be fortunate enough to evaluate—and eventually select from—a number of possible partners.

As one twenty-nine-year-old, never-married woman told me recently, "Let's be honest, the phone isn't ringing off the hook with persistent suitors, so I'm not exactly in a position to be selective or choosy."

Like this woman, many singles wrongly assume that if there is only one choice, they don't need to make a determination—much less make an early-on decision. Since there is no need for efficiency, they falsely infer that they can just bide their time, go with the flow, and see where the relationship ends up. But with this kind of thinking, you'll end up without a well-defined image of your ideal mate . . . and you may end up stuck in an unhappy, unsatisfying marriage for the rest of your life.

We'll discuss all of this in detail later, but for now, let me lead you in what I believe to be a significant direction. In an effort to get your thinking straightened out, I want you to imagine that your list of candidates *is* long. Suppose that your calendar is filled with upcoming dates, singles events, and parties where you'll become acquainted with several eligible people. What's more, assume you already have two or three relationships that could develop into something serious. (I suspect you like this exercise!)

Now your challenge is simple: You need to be able to make an accurate and rapid-fire decision about the best person for you to marry, someone with whom you could be happy for a lifetime. When you're able to do this, you will be on your way to mastering the entire dating process.

I was sitting at a baseball game the other night with my friend Steve, who has never married. He has all kinds of attractive qualities, and he is genuinely liked and pursued by members of the opposite sex. We were chatting about the excitement and the perils of dating. I eventually posed an imaginary dilemma for him that I've been pondering and researching for months. It went like this:

"Steve, assume that I found ten women in your age category who are all single and willing to date you. They are equally good-looking, equally intelligent, and they have equally attractive personalities. But let's say that I have determined ahead of time that marriage to *five* of these persons will prove to be disastrous. They perhaps are emotionally unhealthy or in some other way incapable of a long-term, unselfish, and committed relationship. The other five of these persons are unusually healthy, and marriage to any one of them would have great potential for success."

I knew I had Steve's attention, so I continued. "Now

let's say that you can date each of these ten women two times. And then it is your task to determine which five would be the 'good' choices and which would be the 'bad' choices. Do you think you could identify those persons with whom marriage would likely be disastrous and those with whom marriage would likely be wonderfully positive?"

Steve thought for a while and then said: "Well, I think I'd be right more often than I'd be wrong."

"Steve, this is your future we're talking about!" I chided. "What if you're fooled? What if you just happen to be wrong instead of right for this crucial decision? Are you going to leave the most important decision of your life to chance?"

Steve laughed. "All right, all right, Neil. Get to the point."

"Okay," I said, "what if I told you that based on my research and years of experience as a psychologist, I've come up with a simple, clearly defined process for determining with *certainty* which of those five would be worth pursuing and which would not? Not only that, but what if you could achieve this in two dates or less? Would you be interested in learning these techniques?"

"You bet I would!" Steve said.

So how about you? Would you like to learn to identify—within the span of two dates—if someone is a good
marriage candidate or not? If so, stick with me.

BE SMARTER SO YOU CAN BE HAPPIER

Hardly anyone on earth would argue with me when I
say that your choice of a marriage partner is an overwhelmingly important decision in your life. But listen to
my further assertion: You not only want to make a bril-
liant final decision about the person you marry, but you
also want to be able to make smaller decisions along the
way, quickly and wisely. We'll talk about why "quickly"
is so important a little later, but I want to tell you what
both "quickly" and "wisely" require of you.

In short, you have to be smarter in order to be quicker
and wiser. Being smarter involves a deep understanding of
who you are, what you need from another person in order
to be truly fulfilled, and how you can read critical cues in
other people so you will rapidly know whether they are
right for you. This book is designed to help you get fifty
IQ points smarter about these three subjects.

If both you and the person you're dating agree that
your relationship is casual, informal, and not at all likely
to lead to anything serious and committed, a decision

about continuing to go out together becomes less critical. But if either of you is eager to find a lifelong partner, and if you want to avoid nettlesome entanglements in "going-nowhere" relationships, an early decision about whether to "continue the pursuit" becomes far more important.

A decision to stop dating someone is hard to make, but it should be made as early in the process as possible. In other words, if a new relationship is likely to evolve in a negative direction, the earlier you can end it and move on the better. There are three reasons for this:

First, any developing relationship creates expectations and raises hopes. These hopes and expectations contribute to a significant amount of emotional bonding. When a dating relationship goes on for very long, it often produces in one or both persons strong feelings. Should the relationship end, the person who holds these feelings will be deeply wounded. If a decision to discontinue a dating relationship is eventually going to be made, it is best to make it early on, when emotional ties are not so advanced and complicated.

Second, a relationship that is going nowhere should be ended so both individuals can move on to better prospects. I have seen many relationships prolonged that should have ended far earlier—because the two persons didn't have the courage to stop the relationship when it was obviously heading toward stagnation or catastrophe. As time passes, these relationships become more and more difficult to terminate. They become like quicksand: the deeper you sink, the tougher it is to get out. Far too often, these unacknowledged or unfaced difficulties are never corrected, and the couple end up getting married. Many unhappily married couples have told me that they knew early in the dating relationship it made no sense for them to continue, but they just couldn't bring themselves to hurt the other person or to deny their own desperate desire to be married.

Third, ending a relationship sooner rather than later saves precious time. This is a vital issue for both men and women, particularly as age becomes a factor. I find that women are especially sensitive to wasting time and letting their biological clock tick. Why fritter away valuable weeks, months, or even years in a relationship that will end at some point anyway? It's far better to move on in order to provide maximal opportunity to find someone with whom your chances for marriage are greater.

A DECISION TO CONTINUE DATING ALSO HAS ADVANTAGES

Just as there are critical implications for ending a relationship, deciding to move forward also holds important considerations. First, making a *conscious decision* to continue—rather than just drifting on from week to week— contributes significantly to your positive attitude and demeanor. And, equally important, nothing is quite as attractive to your dating partner as knowing you have carefully weighed the information at hand and have chosen to pursue the relationship.

Obviously, this kind of decision must be the result of a disciplined, purposeful, fully informed process. When the choice to move forward is well thought out and authentic, it has a powerful effect on both persons. And when both the man and the woman detect the same level of thoughtful "positiveness" in each other, the relationship is infused with energy. For instance, the man who forthrightly asks a woman for a third date and hears a hearty "Yes, I'd be delighted" will be as powerfully impacted by her response as she is by his. Their mutual enthusiasm will multiply the bonding effect.

The second positive result of an early, deliberate decision to proceed has to do with momentum. In virtually every relationship, there are complex dynamics. The woman has mixed observations about the man she's dating: "He talks too much, but he's very bright. His life revolves around sports, but he makes me laugh a lot. He is a little more emotionally distant than I would prefer, but he's tender when he talks about his family."

Likewise, the man has both positive and negative impressions of the woman: "She wasn't ready when I came by for her, but she was worth the wait—she looked terrific. She seems a little too eager to find out about my education and employment, but she's easy to be around, and her 'credentials' are impressive. She tries too hard to zero in on my feelings and my 'deep, inner meanings,' but she seems willing to lighten up when I send her signals to back off a little."

So when this fellow asks the woman for a third date and she happily accepts, the two of them implicitly decide to focus on the positive impressions they have of each other rather than the negative. Whether they know it or not, two things will almost surely result: Their decision will evoke more of these positive attributes in the other person by reinforcing them; and even more important, both partners will establish a tendency within themselves to concentrate on the perceived *assets* of their partner rather than the perceived *deficits*.

Remember this: We often have both positive and negative thoughts and feelings at important decision points, and when we elect to go with either the positive or the negative, we will influence our future choices in the same direction. Moreover, we will influence the choices our dating partners make as they watch closely for clues about how we respond to them. So, if a particular relationship deserves to move forward, being positive early on will make it far more likely to advance along that successful trajectory.

WHAT TYPE OF PERSON WOULD YOU LIKE TO MARRY?

In order to make a wise and swift decision about continuing a dating relationship, you must have a well-developed picture of the person you are looking for. You need to know in great detail the type of individual who would be a great mate for you.

I believe that all men and women have the image of their perfect person somewhere in their brain. While it may not be so conscious that they can immediately detail every feature and quality, the image does become more clear and defined if you line up five or ten members of the opposite sex and ask the individual to choose the one with whom they would like to spend more time.

At my seminars, I often describe a research exercise that most single people find fascinating. It goes like this: Imagine yourself in a room with twenty-five members of the opposite sex, all single and all your age. I'll leave you in the room with these twenty-five persons, and you have three minutes to talk with each of them about anything you want. Then at the end of seventy-five minutes, I will come back to the room and take you over to a quiet corner, where I'll ask: "Do you want to get better acquainted with any of these people?"

If you are like the typical person who goes through this exercise, you will point out three to five of them. In which case I would ask, "How in the world did you eliminate twenty to twenty-two of these persons after only three minutes?"

I tell my seminar attendees at some length about how this elimination process occurs for most people. It begins with an ever-present image in their head—a highly detailed picture of the person with whom they would like to spend their lives. Then when they meet each new member of the opposite sex, they compare the real person with this image. Their brain makes hundreds of comparisons, and they end up with a "determination of fit," what I call a bottom-line matching number that informs their eventual decision. My view of "attraction," then, involves a high degree of overlap of their experience with a real person and the wished-for image in their heads.

The question always gets raised about the trustworthiness of these largely unconscious images. If they are so powerful in determining the degree of attraction, we would like to have full confidence in their validity and reliability. That is, we would hope that when a person finds someone much like "the person of their dreams," they would get married and live happily ever after.

Unfortunately, I have little confidence that these perfect-person images will lead you to a great marriage partner. Your images are the result of a thousand influences from untrustworthy sources. At the top of the list is television, which the average high school senior will have watched for twelve thousand hours. Television is a powerful medium, but it is overwhelmingly unreliable when it comes to helping you identify the kind of person with whom you could be happy for a lifetime.

That's where this book comes in. After more than thirty years of helping thousands of people find the love of their life, I believe I know how you should go about the "image-building" process.

GET TO KNOW YOURSELF
EXTREMELY WELL

The right person for you to marry will depend almost totally on who you are. So if you go out and "select" Mr.

or Miss Right before you figure out your own identity, you may end up with a fine person—but not the best match *for you*. (That's why Chapter 2 offers specific principles for getting to know yourself far better than you've ever known yourself before.) If you take this challenge seriously, you will have taken the most important step of all.

It took me a long time to realize the importance of self-awareness. I'm the youngest of three children, and my two sisters are eighteen and eleven years older than I am. To say that I was a "mistake" is a vast understatement. Because I came along so late in my parents' child-rearing years, I was totally spoiled. But I was also emotionally lonely and maybe even emotionally neglected. I always did well in school, but not because I applied myself. I lacked the kind of emotional solidity and stability that allows one to really apply himself.

Still, in the midst of my early insecurities and self-esteem confusion, I showed moments of promise. I had unusually gifted and loyal friends, I displayed academic flashes of ability, developed interpersonal qualities that opened dozens of doors, and could articulate my ideas clearly in front of groups, even when I was young.

So based on all this, what kind of a wife did I need? Let me suggest a few qualities: First, I required someone I respected, as I did my friends, but someone who wouldn't threaten me emotionally. I was too insecure to deal with an overly powerful person, and I was in need of someone whose partnership would help me feel better about myself.

Moreover, since I traveled with a bright crowd, I needed to marry someone I thought of as smart and intellectually quick. And my dad had bred a lot of ambition into me, so I needed someone as ambitious as I was, and someone who would appreciate and share my dreams.

What's more, I grew up attending a church that exerted enormous pressure on all its members to act and believe in very set ways. The leaders were so sure of their absolute rightness that they threatened to reject anyone who wouldn't buy every principle to which they subscribed. Many of their principles seemed unacceptable to me, and on some level of my inner being, I resolved that I would never marry someone from this church.

Understand that as a young person, I was not aware of all these requirements. In fact, I was as unclear about myself and what I needed in a spouse as most people are. Nevertheless, my wife, Marylyn, and I have had a long and remarkable marriage. She has all of those qualities that I so desperately needed. We celebrated our fortieth anniversary recently, and I was struck again with how fortunate and blessed we are to have chosen each other when we lacked any comprehension of why we were doing so. We realize now that our marital success was based largely on sheer luck, not good decision making.

If we were lucky, most people who stumble blindly into marriage are not. In fact, of all the marriages that begin this year, 60 percent will end in separation or divorce. The good news is, you don't have to rely on luck. All the tools, resources, and guidance are available to help you make a wise, fully informed decision about whom to marry.

CREATING YOUR "SHOPPING LIST" FOR A GREAT MATE

By the time you finish this book, you will have a twenty-item checklist of the right person for you. Some items on this list will allow you some flexibility, and others won't. For instance, you may *wish* to find someone whose age is within ten years of your own, but you may *require* a person whose values are almost exactly like yours.

You must discover every single critical factor that will determine whether or not you can experience long-term fulfillment with a person. You can know these things ahead of time! I will help you figure out each of them on the basis of who you are and what you need to be happy.

Daters who don't have the slightest idea of what they're "shopping for" create enormous pain. And there's simply no need to be a sloppy marital shopper. Every question you need to pursue is in this book. If you will read these chapters carefully, modify them for your personal use, and put them into practice at every turn on the road to marriage, your chances of finding the person of your dreams, avoiding the pain of a broken marriage, and making this happen at an early point in your life will be maximized.

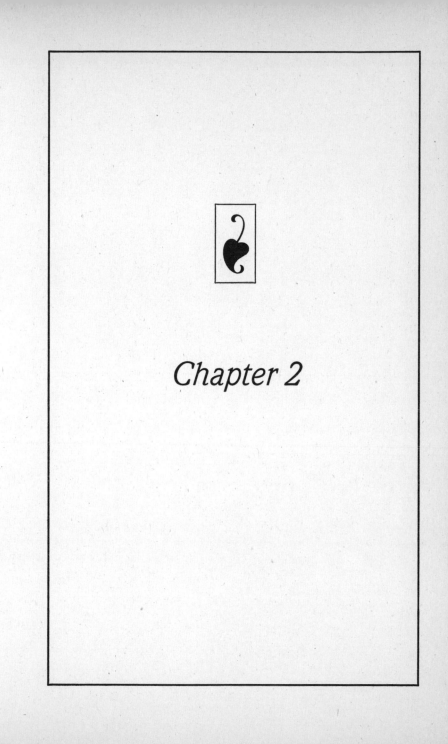

Chapter 2

KNOW
YOURSELF

Mark and Gina came to see me on a chilly, rainy afternoon. The weather outside seemed to match the mood in my counseling office when this couple plopped down on the couch across from me. Their whole demeanor was frosty and frigid.

"What brings you in for therapy?" I asked them.

They looked at each other, and then Mark spoke. "To put it bluntly, we're miserable. We've been married four years, and every day has been a challenge. We're wondering if we should even keep trying."

I asked Gina if that was the way she saw it.

"I'm afraid so," she replied. "About two days after we returned from the honeymoon, we both had the sickening feeling that we had made a huge mistake. It was obvious that we shouldn't be together. It's been downhill since then."

As our session unfolded, Mark and Gina told a story I've heard dozens of times from marriage partners in peril. After a blissful courtship, they married and almost immediately discovered vast differences. They were opposites when it came to communication style, conflict resolution, personal habits, and a few dozen other qualities that come to light when you live with someone. Somehow all these differences were pushed aside and ignored amid their initial intoxicating feelings of infatuation.

So they ended up in my office, attempting to figure out how a relationship that held such promise could plummet to the depths of drudgery.

Gina said something that day I wish every single person could hear and grasp:

"I realize now that I had no idea who I was before I got married. I was thirty years old, and I just wanted to get married while I had the chance. Mark was a nice guy who had a good job and came from a solid family. I figured, *What more could a girl want?* Unfortunately, I had only the vaguest notion of my deep longings, my unique personality traits, my strengths and weaknesses. And since I didn't know who I was, I didn't have a clue about the kind of person I needed for a partner."

As this couple painfully discovered, you can't select the right person to marry until you know precisely who you are—unless you're lucky! But nobody should rely on luck when it comes to a decision that will determine who your financial partner for life will be, who your roommate for life will be, who will be the joint parent of every child you have . . . and ten thousand other crucial matters. You can make a great choice of a marriage partner— and the place to start is with a careful understanding of exactly who you are.

I am convinced that you can develop such a clarity of thinking that after only two dates with a person, you will be fully confident about whether to proceed or not. If you master the five strategies outlined in this chapter, every part of the dating process will become decidedly easier.

Be in Touch with Yourself

When I was an adolescent, I knew very little about myself. Oh sure, I knew I loved sports, steak, and a good practical joke. But I was oblivious to anything beyond superficial likes and dislikes. Most young people are in the same boat. Their identity process is a long way from being complete. And until they identify themselves in a precise and detailed way, they are in no position to identify that person who will be able to move through life with them like two professional dancers moving perfectly in relation to each other.

Don't think that when you move out of adolescence and into your twenties that your identity naturally takes shape. In our culture, the identifying process usually requires most of the first twenty-five to twenty-eight years of life. That's why I encourage young people not to get married too early. They haven't yet "grown into themselves." Their personality cement hasn't hardened at that point. In fact, the one statistic that never fails to hit me with a jolt is this: The divorce rate for those who marry at twenty-one or twenty-two is exactly *double* that of those who marry at twenty-four or twenty-five. Self-identity has to be the reason.

Sometimes the self-identifying task takes even longer than twenty-eight years. It's not uncommon for two middle-aged persons to marry with little understanding of who they are as individuals. But when your identity process is well developed—when you are clearly in touch with the person you truly are—the task of selecting the right marriage partner becomes significantly easier.

Let's say you are a person with unbridled energy. You like to go, go, go all the time. You need someone with an energy level close to yours. In fact, this is one of the differences that drove Mark and Gina to my therapy office (and drove both of them crazy!). He loved to get out of the house and do things—attend sporting events, go to movies, play pickup basketball with his pals. Gina, however, enjoyed quiet dinners followed by a leisurely evening of reading. Her perfect Saturday would be to putter around in her garden, sip iced tea on the porch, and rent a movie (preferably a nice, slow romantic film) at night. Mark acquiesced to Gina's wishes a few times—and his nervous energy caused him to nearly go insane. Before long, they made a tacit agreement to "do their own thing." While Gina dawdled around the house, Mark went to the batting cages, caught the new Schwarzenegger movie with his buddies, and polished off the day at the Monster Truck Show at the local racetrack. Mark and Gina's worlds hardly ever intersected, and they became strangers to each other.

Of course, energy level is only one of a hundred important qualities to consider about yourself and a potential mate. Intelligence is another. A marriage doesn't work well when one person is significantly more intelligent than the other. Imagine the degree of satisfaction a couple will achieve if the wife enjoys pondering the writings of Nietzsche and Hegel, while her husband is challenged by X-Men comic books. Or if a man loves to dissect and debate theological issues and his wife never gives a thought to such matters, they will likely become frustrated with each other. This is not to suggest that people with higher intelligence have better marriages—not at all. The important thing is the match-up of people with *similar* levels of intelligence.

Also consider interests and hobbies. Do you like classical music? Or jazz? Or country? Whatever your musical preferences, having someone who shares them will be important to a good marital partnership. Becoming clear about each of your interests will give you additional information about yourself—and additional confidence that you know what you're looking for when you're dating.

Of course, it's just as critical to know what you don't like. If baseball bores you to tears, you don't want to marry someone who spends six months a year playing it, watching it, talking about it, and debating it. Or if you love to attend the theater and your partner falls asleep as soon as the curtain goes up, you're in for trouble.

The more you know about yourself, the clearer will be your sense of inner direction when it comes to finding the love of your life. With increased knowledge about your physical, emotional, intellectual, and spiritual qualities, your skillfulness as a mate selector will soar. People who find dating confusing and bewildering almost always lack familiarity with themselves.

How to Get to Know Yourself

All people are incredibly complex. There are so many parts to all of us, and marriage often brings these various parts into play. The challenge of getting married is first and foremost the challenge of studying yourself and becoming well aware of all the special features that combine to make you the unique individual you are. What follows are five practical strategies for learning about yourself.

STRATEGY 1: ANSWER THESE TWENTY QUESTIONS

Write at least one paragraph in response to each of the following twenty questions:

1. Who is the most important person in your life, and why?

2. What is the one dream for your life you most look forward to achieving?

3. Who has the capacity to make you angrier than anyone else in your life, and what in particular does he or she do to make you angry?

4. Who has the capacity to make you feel loved more than anyone else in your life, and what in particular does he or she do to cause you to feel so lovable?

5. What is it like being you? More precisely, how do you feel about yourself—physically, emotionally, mentally, and spiritually?

6. When do you feel inspired? Who and what contribute to your sense of inspiration? How does it feel when you are inspired?

7. What is the most important thing in the world to you?

8. If you had one day to live, how would you want to spend it?

9. When do you feel most afraid?

10. If you could accomplish only one thing during the rest of your life, what would it be?

11. What bores you? What always bores you, and what never bores you?

12. How important is money to you? How much time do you spend thinking about it, and what income level do you aspire to?

13. What is the role of God in your life? Do you believe there is a God, and if so, what is God like in relation to you?

14. In order, what are your three strongest interests?

15. Who is your biggest enemy, and precisely how and why did this person become your enemy?

16. How important is food to you? Do you think of it very often, and do you feel disciplined in your management of food intake?

17. Does the idea of being married to the same person for the rest of your life sound appealing to you—or not so appealing? What is there about it that you would especially like or not like?

18. Do you think of yourself as an emotionally healthy person? In what ways are you especially healthy, and in what ways could you use improvement?

19. What is the role of conflict in your life? Do you argue or fight very much with the people closest to you? How does it usually turn out for you?

20. What specifically would you like your closest
friends to say about you at your funeral?

If I could hear your answers to these twenty questions, I would come to know you well. But, of course,
it's not me who needs to know you—it's you! I'm convinced that anyone who seriously responds to these
questions—in writing—will gain a world of new insight
into themselves.

So start with this first exercise. Take an evening to do
it well. I guarantee that by the end of the evening, you will
be impressed with how much of the inside you gets lifted
to the surface of your awareness.

STRATEGY 2: DISCUSS YOUR ANSWERS WITH TWO OR
THREE CLOSE FRIENDS OR FAMILY MEMBERS

Let's be honest—sometimes other people can see us
more clearly than we can see ourselves. We all have blind
spots, and we're all shortsighted about certain aspects of
our personality. Therefore, the purpose of this second
exercise is to solicit open and honest feedback from the
people who know you best. This kind of input is richest
when you give each of these important people plenty of
material to discuss.

Ask three people—people who know you well—for an

hour of their time. Tell them exactly what you're trying to do: to get to know yourself better than you've ever known yourself before. Let them know that you're reading this book, that you've just finished answering twenty challenging questions, and that you would appreciate their excruciatingly honest feedback. Tell them you want to read them your answers, and then you would like them to add anything that gives a more complete picture or point out anything that doesn't ring true. You will probably need to assure these people that you have "thick skin" and that your friendship or relationship with them can handle their honest feedback.

When it comes to getting to know yourself, friends and family members who know you well can contribute enormously. They often have a perspective of you that you don't have, and frequently, their perspective has never been shared with you. Sometimes it is this information that triggers a whole new set of insights for you, and these insights may lead you to search for a person different from the one you had previously pursued.

STRATEGY 3: DEVELOP YOUR FAMILY TREE, COMPLETE WITH PROFILES OF YOUR PRIMARY FAMILY MEMBERS

For better or worse, all of us are largely products of our families. We are shaped, molded, and formed in thousands of ways by our parents, siblings, and extended family members. Sometimes we're influenced by forebears whom we didn't even know. I never met my maternal grandparents, but I certainly heard a lot about them from my mother and my uncles. I've come to realize that these grandparents contributed a great deal to making me who I am today. As a matter of fact, I often think about my grandmother and grandfather, and I suddenly get in touch with something that is surprisingly true about them and me.

I know much more about my father's parents. The more I learn about my paternal grandmother and grandfather, the more I start hitting pay dirt in regard to understanding my formation. Then the pay dirt turns to pure gold when I get to my mother and dad. I'm so much like the latter two that I find it shocking. If I want to find out more and more about me, a great place to turn is to the two of them.

For instance, the older I get, the more I remind myself of my dad. Sometimes, in the middle of my doing something new, I step back for a second and sense how much like my dad I have become. I often turn to Marylyn at such moments and ask, "Am I becoming a lot like my dad?" or "Did that seem a lot like my dad right then?" And invariably she answers: "Yes, you are very much like your dad! You always have been, and you're becoming even more so."

My point in all of this is to suggest that a productive way to gain a deeper understanding of yourself is to plot your family tree. Make a circle for each person on a piece of paper. At the top, start as far back in your lineage as possible. My knowledge goes back only to my grandparents, but if you're especially fortunate, yours may go back much farther. Then draw circles for yourself and any siblings you may have. Finally, make a place for each of your children (if you have any).

Next, give a significant amount of thought to each of these persons. What do you know about them that relates directly to you? What were (or are) they like, and how are you similar? The fact is that they have biological and sociological links to you, and chances are that your identity is at least somewhat like theirs.

Finally, select two or three of these persons, and write a page or more about each of them. If I were choosing three persons from my tree, I would select my parents and my maternal grandmother. These are the three who had the greatest influence on me. In my therapy practice, I have never met a single person who didn't find this exercise a generous source of information.

STRATEGY 4: ANALYZE YOUR HISTORY IN FIVE-YEAR
SEGMENTS

At my seminars, I utilize an exercise that has a powerful effect on many of the attendees. I ask everyone to
close their eyes, and then I give them detailed instruc-
tions about how to become deeply relaxed. Once they are
in a relaxed state, I say, "Imagine you are walking down
a country road, and eventually you come to a grassy park
in the middle of a grove of trees. As you saunter through
the park, you come upon a swing attached to a tall tree.
Sitting in the swing is a five-year-old child. As you look
closely at the child, you realize it's you—at five years of
age. You start talking to the child, and you have a dialogue between the 'child you' and the 'grown-up you'."

I then direct the content around which the discussion
takes place. For instance, I ask the audience members to
tell the child what they appreciate about the child, and I
ask the child to share what it was like being them at that
particular time.

As the exercise becomes more and more obviously
productive for the persons involved (there are usually
tears and laughter), I keep taking them down the same
country road where they meet up with "an earlier ver-

sion" of themselves at five-year intervals in their life. I actually participate in the exercise myself, and I am amazed at how much rich, emotional material comes flooding into my consciousness. For instance, I find myself with much sympathy for the confused and frightened fifteen-year-old me; and I am often moved by the obvious passion with which the current me thanks the twenty-year-old me for the courage and determination to work so hard for so many years to make something meaningful possible for my life.

All of us can find out a lot about ourselves by "unpacking" our lives in five-year segments. So I encourage you to take a sheet of paper and begin by writing as much as you can remember about the first five years of your life. Obviously, much of what you write will be what you have found out about your life from others, but you may have several strong memories of that time. Then do the same thing for years six through ten and each succeeding five-year block thereafter.

STRATEGY 5: TAKE ONE OR MORE PSYCHOLOGICAL INVENTORIES

When people come to my office for psychotherapy, I nearly always offer them the opportunity to take one or more psychological inventories. Each of these inventories is designed to shed light on them or on one of their relationships. For nearly every person who comes to me, I suggest the Minnesota Multiphasic Personality Inventory (MMPI). Comprised of 567 true-false questions, it results in an extremely helpful report about the inner makeup of each person. Unfortunately, this inventory has to be taken in conjunction with seeing a professional counselor, but there are other inventories that are self-administered and can be sent for scoring and interpretation.

For persons interested in marriage, I have developed a resource ("The Finding the Love of Your Life Kit"), which has three long, self-scoring inventories to help people gain information about themselves. One of these I call the "bottom-line test," in which people rate themselves from 1 to 10 on a hundred different dimensions. They rate themselves on intelligence, energy, personal habits, and so forth. Then they count up all their individual scores on the one hundred scales, and their bottom-line score will fall between 100 (if they gave themselves a 1 on each dimension) and 1,000 (if they gave themselves a 10 on each).

There are dozens of inventories you can take to find out about yourself, and whichever one you select will be a great help in gaining self-knowledge.

REAP THE REWARD OF
SELF-UNDERSTANDING

The payoff for all this self-discovery and self-aware-ness is simple but profound: Men and women who know themselves well stand an excellent chance of selecting a mate well suited to them. Conversely, those people who are largely unaware of their inner workings make a decision as if they're spinning a roulette wheel—they cross their fingers and hope for the best.

The choice of a well-suited mate is the long-term reward for all this inner exploration, but I hope you see short-term benefits as well. If you know yourself inti-mately, you can quickly and efficiently evaluate your dates to see if they're a good match for you. You can know at an early point in any relationship whether you should continue to invest time, energy, and caring.

Moreover, I hope that you hear in this chapter an enormous amount of hope that you can gain a deep and detailed sense of who you are, that you can develop a pic-ture of yourself that will make the selection of a marriage partner much more likely to be successful, and that, in knowing so much about yourself, you can learn to do all of this with amazing efficiency in the first two dates.

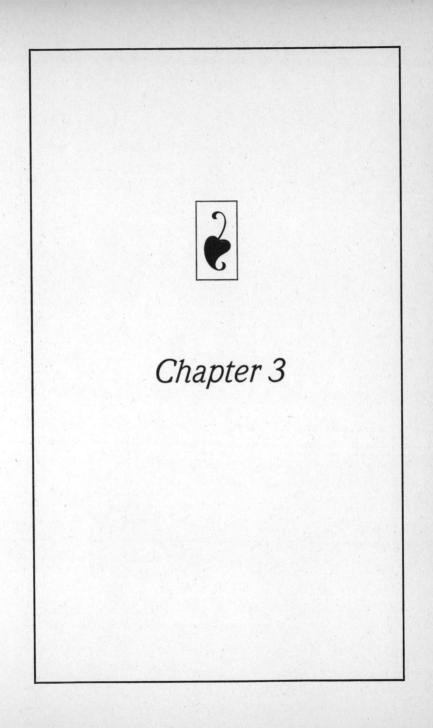

Chapter 3

YOUR MUST-HAVE AND
CAN'T-STAND LISTS

Suppose you could choose ten qualities that the love of your life would have. Which would you choose? But wait—let's sweeten the deal. Not only do you get to select ten positive qualities this special person will have, but you can also identify and eliminate ten deficits. Which twenty items would make your list?

I recently asked these same questions of a twenty-four-year-old single graduate student named Kathryn.

"Oh, I like the sound of this scenario," she said. "This shouldn't be hard, since I've thought a lot about the man of my dreams."

"Good," I replied. "Go ahead and start building your list."

With a far-off look in her eye and a dreamy sound in her voice, she began, "First, he'd have to be intelligent."

You might have guessed a graduate student would put that at the top of the list.

"That's fine," I told her, "but it's too general. Be as specific as possible. How intelligent?"

"About like me," she said.

"Well, how intelligent are you?" I asked.

"Quite a bit higher than average," Kathryn said softly, "but certainly not genius."

"Okay," I said. "What's next?"

We were off and running. In fact, Kathryn nearly used up her limit in her next breath.

"Well," she said, "I need a man who is witty, kind, energetic, emotionally healthy, hard-working, ambitious—"

"Wait! I can't count that fast!" I said. I ran down her list in my mind. "All right, that leaves you just three more."

Then the fun began. She wanted to include a dozen more qualities, but she knew she had to narrow down her list.

"I like someone who dresses nice . . . and has a handsome face . . . and is well groomed . . . Hey, I guess I could group all those things under 'appearance.'"

"Ah, you're pretty clever," I said. "But remember, Kathryn, you have to be specific. Do you want to use those qualities as your last three, or do you want to consider some others?"

She began to agonize. Finally, she sifted and sorted until she had her top ten list. Her list of ten negatives seemed more manageable for her at first. She started with "doesn't smoke, doesn't cheat, doesn't lie, isn't a flake, doesn't intimidate, and doesn't let his anger get out of control." She kept going until she had her ten items, but then I teased her with three or four others.

"What about procrastination? Does that one matter to you? Or sloppiness around the house, or being a mama's boy, a nerd, or a druggie? What about those?"

"Hmmm. I didn't think about those things," she said. "Okay, Neil, let me start over."

"Kathryn, I thought you said this would be easy!" I chided. It took her another ten minutes before she was satisfied with her list.

COMPILING YOUR LISTS

In the last chapter, we talked about the first step to becoming a wise, perceptive, proficient dater—that is, getting to know yourself inside and out. Step two is the

47

exercise I put Kathryn through. It's the process of compiling your top ten positive list and your top ten negative list—or what I call your "must-have" and "can't-stand" lists. Becoming crystal clear about these characteristics will prepare you to be a highly efficient "mate shopper," a person who will know with confidence and clarity after only two dates whether a potential partner is worth more of your time, energy, and caring.

These are the qualities you are going to memorize, literally burn into your brain, and you're going to take them with you on every date you go on until you get married. If you think it's important to have a shopping list when you go to the grocery store, it's a hundred times more important to have your shopping list with you when you go on a date.

A BAD MARRIAGE IS WORSE THAN NO MARRIAGE AT ALL

If you want to get married in the near future, then treat dating like shopping. I don't want to come across as cavalier, because selecting a mate is extremely serious business. My point is, though, that you must know exactly what you're looking for before you go into the "market." Fuzzy thinking leads you down blind alleys and toward dead ends, and before you know what has happened to you, you'll be considering marrying somebody who is a lousy match for you.

Some singles I work with absolutely refuse to build a shopping list. Or if I do convince them to create a list, they refuse to carry it with them when they go out. Here's what they say: "If I can't find a person who meets what I know to be necessary for me to be happy, then maybe I'll need to lower my standards." And here is what they never say but what I'm convinced they mean: "I want to get married! I *need* to get married! Therefore, if I have to settle for less, so be it. After all, a less-than-ideal man (or woman) is better than no man at all."

I argue against this theme with everything I have. I encourage people to figure out the kind of person they need to be really happy and then to hold to this set of criteria to the very end. Otherwise, they could easily end up being part of the marital failure epidemic. Think of it: If present trends continue, two-thirds of all the marriages that begin this year in the United States will end in separation or divorce. And the pain of these broken relationships is beyond description. I absolutely guarantee you that a bad marriage is a thousand times worse than no marriage at all.

WHAT CONSTITUTES A MUST-HAVE OR A CAN'T-STAND FOR YOU?

On the basis of the work you did in the last chapter, what is it that inspires your passion, gets your heart racing, and captivates your total attention? It may be an interest like golf. I have noted that when two people have the same interest, one never calls the other a "fanatic." I have never known a woman who likes golf a lot who also calls herself a "golf widow." I'm convinced that golf widows are women who forgot to put "golf addiction" on their can't-stand list. And now they are stuck with a husband who loves something they don't enjoy at all.

Of course, the husband has the reverse problem. He is head over heels in love with golf, and he forgot to make "loves golf" one of the ten big ones on his must-have list. Now he has to fight for time to play, time to practice, money for lessons and clubs and dues—all because he didn't build his list properly, or didn't hold to it.

When two people fail to overlap on anything really important, all kinds of problems can develop. I know a lot of highly spiritual people—people for whom spiritual pursuits are the most important things in their life. They pray frequently, think a lot about their relationship with God, attend church and Bible classes regularly, and are convinced that the development of their spiritual life matters more than anything else. These people need to put SPIRITUAL PASSION at the top of their must-have list in capital letters.

We could cite hundreds of examples. If you keep your house, car, and desk clean and spotless—and if it's important that your spouse share your passion for neatness—put this on your list. If you hate secondhand smoke, you should put "smoking" on your can't-stand list. If you are superambitious, and if you get bored by complacent, apathetic people, write "must be a go-getter" on your list. If you have a need for fun and laughter, put "great sense of humor" on your list.

Whatever it is that you simply must have, or simply can't stand, you should take these qualities extremely seriously. To "sign on" with a person who lacks some of your necessities or possesses some of your hated deficiencies is to set your marriage up for deep trouble.

WHY LIMIT THE LISTS TO TEN ITEMS?

Since I believe that there are hundreds of qualities you might wish for in a lifetime mate, I put a limit of ten on your lists only for mathematical and practical reasons. Your "pool of candidates" is usually so limited that your chance of finding a person with *every* quality on a list of twenty-five or fifty items is very slim.

Here's what I mean: A woman's pool of possible spouses is comprised of single men she meets at work, church, the gym, her neighborhood, the softball team, and so on. So if a woman says she wants a partner with a college education, she immediately eliminates many of the men she knows. Likewise, if she wants a man free of all addictions and emotional hang-ups, she eliminates another sizable part of the population. With every criterion from her list, her pool of eligible, qualified bachelors shrinks considerably. We would need a mathematician to calculate the total number of persons required in the beginning pool for her to end up with a "Mr. Right" after applying ten rigorous must-haves and ten equally rigorous can't-stands.

"Well, then," you ask, "shouldn't I just cut down my list further—to maybe four or five items—to increase my odds of finding a match?" I suppose you could, but I think you would also increase your odds of ending up in a miserable relationship. If your list is too short, you'll be forced to rely on very few strengths to carry the weight of the relationship—and you will allow for many more deficits that could sink the relationship. A list of ten things you definitely want and ten things you definitely don't want offers a happy medium: you'll be picky enough to ensure your mate will be well suited to you, but not so picky that you'll never find someone who can live up to your demands.

WHAT IF SOMEONE MATCHES UP WITH MOST OF YOUR LIST?

Suppose you've clarified your lists, and you feel confident that the must-haves and can't-stands represent exactly what you want in a spouse. But then you meet someone—a terrific someone—who has, say, eight of your ten positives and only one of your negatives. That's a good batting average, right? So should you pursue the person? I don't think so! I've watched hundreds of people try to make relationships work despite just one or two glaring deviations from their list, and most times they ended up disappointed. I'm not saying that *all* of these marriages turn sour, but the vast majority do.

For instance, think about the man for whom economic stability is essential. He works ten or twelve hours at his job every day, takes short lunch breaks so he can get more done, dreams of buying a home, saves all the money he can, and considers frugality a prized virtue. Then he meets a woman who is pretty, intelligent, highly spiritual, neat, and emotionally healthy. Unfortunately, she isn't frugal—indeed, she spends quite freely and always has. Can this man make a marriage work with her? I doubt it. If frugality and thrift are, in fact, central to his goals and lifestyle, the issue would become a wedge between this couple. She will drive him nuts with her shopping sprees, her generosity to every cause she encounters, her desire for clothes and gifts, and her need for economic freedom.

Or think about the woman who gains most of her meaning in life from conversation with close friends and family. Communication is nourishment for her soul just as food is for her body. When she goes for very long without connection with someone, she shrinks at the center of herself—just as her body would shrink if she went without food for any period of time. Then she meets a good man who has always described himself as a "private person." He conducts his life from a small headquarters deep within himself to which only he can gain access. He works hard, earns a respectable living, is highly moral, and doesn't have any major personality flaws. He just never feels comfortable revealing his innermost thoughts and feelings to others.

You can predict what would happen if these two got married. The woman would die a lonely death with this man. Her natural eagerness to share her life, to merge with him, to participate in the give-and-take of verbal interaction would leave her feeling frustrated and unfulfilled. He might try his best, even listen to self-improvement tapes and attend seminars, but his best efforts would likely fall short. They could both be saved incalculable pain if she wrote COMMUNICATOR at the top of her must-have list.

Marriage failures are frequently the result of rationalizing away a must-have or a can't-stand item. Pretending that you can "get over it" may work for a while, but not forever. Insisting that those "eight great qualities make up for the missing two" won't wash in the long run. To move ahead with a relationship because someone "comes closer to fulfilling the list than anyone else" is a recipe for pain and heartache. Your must-haves and can't-stands—if thoughtfully and accurately identified—will be as important in ten or twenty years from now as they are today.

MUST YOU HOLD OUT FOR PERFECTION?

I have never encountered a perfect marriage. Marylyn and I have what I call an "A" marriage, but it is a long way from perfection. Our relationship is mutually satisfying because we fit each other's list to a tee. Nevertheless, there are times when we squabble, get huffy, and annoy each other.

When couples come to see me for counseling, I often meet with the partners individually so I can get "their side of the story" unfiltered and uninterrupted. I've talked to thousands of men about their wives, and I've talked at a later time to those wives under the same confidential conditions. In the marriages that were working pretty well, I've heard about perceived imperfections that were not viewed as "marriage killers." Husbands will frequently say something like, "I wish Karen wasn't so nitpicky and uptight about housecleaning, but I've learned to adapt to her style, and it's not really a problem anymore." And wives might say something along these lines: "Rick is such a tightwad. I've got to justify every penny I spend. But to be honest, it's not a big deal." Almost every marriage has irritations and imperfections—and those things we can adjust to and learn to live with. But a marriage killer is a quality that relates directly to an item on one person's must-have or can't-stand list.

For instance, some people can be happy with mates who have little ambition. It just isn't crucial to them. For someone else, this same low level of ambition in their mate would be a significant turnoff and constant frustration. The possession of drive and determination as a quality is sometimes critical and sometimes of virtually no importance. What are simply *imperfections* in some marriages are *killers* in others. All marriages have some imperfections, but few marriages can survive any killers.

Some people falsely believe that finding a spouse who fits their list ensures perpetual bliss. The most wonderful person in the world still gets grumpy and grouchy. Even when you find the person who satisfies all ten of your must-haves and has none of your ten can't-stands, there will still be imperfections in your relationship. Her mood will sometimes be chilly and distant. He will sometimes procrastinate doing his chores and keeping his promises. She will spend more for her new dress than you had expected. He will sign up for still another bowling league. She will tell her mother more of your family problems than you would like. He will talk more glowingly about his secretary than you feel comfortable with. She won't have dinner ready on time; he won't take his turn fixing dinner.

The bottom line is this: Does he have all your must-haves? Is she free of all your can't-stands? If you can honestly say that this is the case, your marriage is likely to do quite well, however many annoyances the two of you experience. In fact, you show me a couple in which both people can honestly say that their must-have and can't-stand lists are being satisfied, and I'll show you a man and a woman who almost assuredly enjoy a supremely delightful marriage.

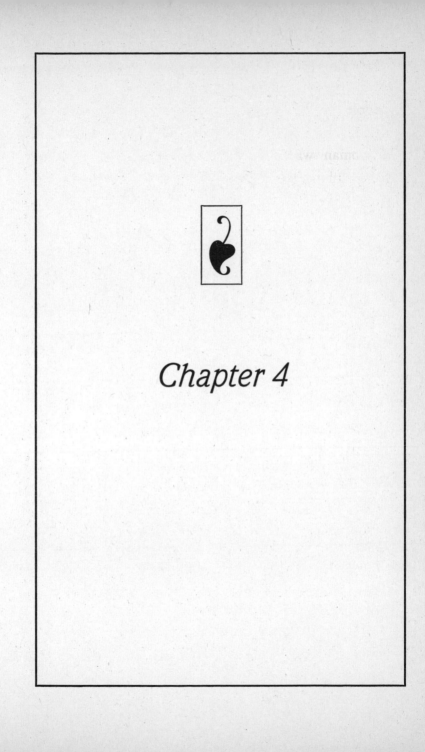

Chapter 4

HOW TO READ
SOMEONE LIKE A BOOK

Imagine that you are on a first date, and the evening is just getting started. You are set for a three- or four-hour experience together—dinner at a nice restaurant, followed by a concert at a local club. You and your date are both nervous because you don't know each other well, and you want to make a good impression. Nevertheless, you're finding it easy to be in the other person's company, and the conversation is flowing smoothly and naturally. You think to yourself, *It's too soon to tell what will develop, but this looks promising.*

You're off to a good start. All the signs look positive. So what can you do during the rest of the evening—and perhaps on your second date—to help yourself decide whether to continue dating this person?

We've talked in the previous chapters about the

importance of getting to know yourself well and listing qualities you want and don't want in another person. Now, in step three, your goal is to collect as much information as possible related to your lists. In the middle of a scene like the one I just described, your challenge will be to keep your antennae up so you can discern how well this man or woman matches up with your must-haves and can't-stands.

INFORMATION FLOWS FREELY
DURING A DATE

It may seem overly simplistic to suggest that every person "announces" hundreds of things about themselves over the course of a three- or four-hour date. But if you are a keen and intentional observer, you'll be amazed at how much information you can gather. At the end of your first date, you can know enough about another person to make a wise decision about ending the relationship or moving ahead.

If you're serious about knowing whether someone is worth pursuing in two dates or less, your primary goal will be to watch for clues and cues from the other person. I'm not trying to spoil all the fun by turning a date into a reconnaissance mission. Of course you want to have an enjoyable time. But if your fundamental focus is determining the wisdom of pursuing a particular person, you will take this fact-finding objective seriously.

What's more, I encourage singles not to get caught up in trying to impress or "win over" their date. If you're too concerned about your own presentation and performance, you'll fail to discern all the necessary information from the other person. It's only natural to want to make a good impression, but mature dating involves questioning deeper matters—matters that determine the likelihood of a healthy, long-term match.

LEARNING TO BE "OTHER-CONSCIOUS"

If you learn to pay close attention to all the cues you receive during the first and second dates, you will end up with a mountain of data. In order to do this observing well, though, you will need to be secure within yourself, because accurate observation always starts with "getting beyond yourself." I often tell singles, "To really get to know someone, you have to stop being *self*-conscious and learn to be *other*-conscious."

Obviously, dating can produce lots of anxiety. This anxiety usually relates to your concern about how you are coming across—what kind of impression you're making.

It is immensely important to feel comfortable enough within yourself that you can pay close attention to the other person. How do you do this? How do you achieve internal calm and confidence when you are "interviewing" for the most significant role in your life?

This question, of course, is closely related to the larger issue of how emotionally healthy you are. And the answer begins with how secure you feel deep within yourself. I will talk about all this in much greater detail in a later chapter, but it boils down to a crucial consideration: If you don't feel secure within yourself, you may not be ready to start a serious dating relationship.

HONING YOUR OBSERVATIONAL POWERS

If you want to gain maximum information from another person, get him or her talking—and then listen carefully. Asking key questions is critical to the process. These questions can begin with something as innocuous as "How is your life going these days?" or "What do you enjoy most about living in Norfolk?"

Then as you listen to what the person says, you can ask follow-up questions in a natural way, and you can move toward more meaningful topics. You want to discover what the person enjoys about his daily experience, whether he is happy and why, how much his job means to him, and how involved he is at church or in other community activities.

Pay close attention to information about family background, especially the relationships the person has with his or her parents. As a matter of fact, I suspect there is no more important information available than that which reveals the depth and quality of these two primary relationships. Similarly, you should want to know about the quality of the parents' marriage. It is good to know as much as you can about whether the parents enjoy each other or simply tolerate each other.

While bombarding your date with one question after another would be inappropriate, any person who listens well and asks thoughtful questions will almost always be seen as caring and sensitive. It was Dale Carnegie, author of one of the all-time best-selling books, *How to Win Friends and Influence People*, who said that individuals are rated as great communicators when they take an active interest in getting to know the other person. And it is getting to know the other person that provides you with the information on which to base a decision about continuing a relationship.

One final word about listening. There is nothing in the world that conveys honor and caring as effectively as active listening. To improve your interpersonal skills immediately, begin practicing the art of listening. Here are some simple suggestions:

- Look at the other person and make consistent eye contact.

- Acknowledge when you hear and understand what's been said by reflecting the person's message. That is, repeat in your own words what you heard the person say.

- Empathize. Try to stand in the person's shoes and see things from his or her perspective. This will show that you care about what your date says and feels.

- Try not to judge what is said. Remain open-minded and receptive. Nothing shuts down communication faster than a judgmental attitude.

These efforts will both promote your relationship with the other person and provide you with plenty of information. Then your decision as to whether or not you should pursue them will be so much better grounded in fact and reality.

BE ATTENTIVE TO BEHAVIOR AS WELL AS WORDS

A person will usually speak volumes about himself through the way he acts, and your alertness to behavior will give you considerable data for your eventual decision. For instance, the first telephone call will in itself be critical. If you are on the receiving end, you will want to ask yourself about the appropriateness of the call's timing, the degree of courtesy accorded you, the freedom you are given to respond, the thoughtfulness of the planning, and the kindness you experience.

If you are the caller, similar observations should be made. How well is your call received? How sensitive is the person to the difficulty involved in risking the call? Does the person respond with appreciation? Does she come across as coy and elusive?

Then when you're on the date, behavior is especially informative. Is the person punctual? Are you treated with courtesy? Does your date seem comfortable or uptight? Also, watch things such as the person's driving for cues about interpersonal style. Does he drive within reasonable limits? Or does he drive too fast, take too many chances, seem too much in a hurry, and generally make you feel uncomfortable?

If you go out to eat, does your date treat the server kindly? Does he or she use good manners? And is the restaurant appropriate to the occasion? All of these provide important facts about the other person.

LOOK FOR INFORMATION THAT RELATES TO ITEMS ON YOUR LISTS

Your information-gathering activities should relate directly to the must-haves and the can't-stands on your list. If you must have a person who shares your interest in the arts, you will want to move the conversation in that direction. If ambition is a must for you, bring the conversation around to career and personal aspirations. If spirituality is important, focus attention on that area.

Some items on your can't-stand list will be easy to assess; others may be difficult. For instance, if you can't stand smoking, it shouldn't be hard to get information on that subject. But if you're adamant about never marrying a person with an addiction, let me assure you that information about addictions may lie in hiding until the second *year* of dating. That's part of the reason why I encourage a couple to go together for two years before they decide to marry. It often takes that long to know everything you need to know about another person, especially when you are considering making a lifetime commitment.

One final note on gathering information in relation to your list. When I am working with people in psychotherapy, I try to help them build an "airtight" list. This means that no item should be on the must-have and can't-stand lists if it is not a "relationship killer." When you have airtight lists, any information that reveals the absence of a positive asset or the presence of a negative one means only one thing—the end of that dating relationship. Far too many people go hurtling through this roadblock with rationalizations that are baffling and, ultimately, self-sabotaging. You may be tempted to continue dating a person even if it becomes obvious that he or she does not possess one of your must-haves or does possess one of your can't-stands. You must not allow this to happen. It almost never spells anything other than more heartache—for both of you.

ASSESSING YOUR DATE'S JUDGMENT

One of the most important qualities that any person brings to a relationship is good judgment. If the individual knows how to make consistently wise decisions, he or she will almost certainly contribute consistently to the strength and health of the relationship. So your task becomes one of "judging your date's judgments."

Good or bad judgments will become obvious all along the way. That's why I stressed earlier such things as the timing of the first call. Timing involves a judgment. And the way each person presents himself during that call demonstrates other judgments. The selection of the dating activity is the result of still another judgment. The amount of caution or recklessness when driving offers still more clues about judgment.

During almost every three- or four-hour date, there will arise many situations that will involve a person's judgment. I encourage you to watch for these and to log away in your brain the essential judgment qualities that you will assess when the date is over.

DO YOU FEEL FREE TO BE YOURSELF?

I believe that your own contentment requires that you be authentically yourself. You will never be able to experience inner wholeness and peace if you fall short of being the person you truly are. Thus, it is absolutely crucial that you feel complete freedom to be yourself with the person with whom you will spend the rest of your life.

If you are like me, you feel different degrees of freedom with different people. With some persons, you experience a kind of total acceptance and unconditional affirmation that sets you free at a deep and fundamental level. With others, you feel a need to live up to their expectations, preferences, and strongly held opinions.

This issue of freedom is so important to the development of a healthy relationship that I lift it up for special attention. If you and your partner do not have the freedom to be fully and authentically yourselves, the relationship is sure to remain unfulfilling. But if you do feel this freedom, and if you know how to live and grow within it, all kinds of meaningful relational consequences are sure to evolve.

STAY INWARDLY SECURE AND OUTWARDLY ALERT

If you are able to master your own anxiety so that you can attend to all the clues your date provides, this flow of information will greatly assist you in determining whether the requirements of your lists can be satisfied in this new relationship.

Remember, if you gain clear information indicating that you cannot find in this person what you need to have in a lifetime mate, the best time to terminate is as early as possible—before expectations are raised and emotional ties start forming.

On the other hand, if all the information you gather increases your confidence that this person may possess all your must-haves and none of your can't-stands, you are in a position to move the relationship forward decisively. In a world in which decisiveness is greatly admired and rewarded, you are sure to be a winner either way.

Chapter 5

THE TWENTY-FIVE
MOST POPULAR
MUST-HAVES

At a recent seminar where I spoke on finding the love of your life, a fellow in his late twenties approached me to talk. He was a big, handsome guy who wore a sweatshirt that said UCLA Athletic Department. He looked around to see if anyone was listening, then leaned in close.

"Dr. Warren, I like your idea about creating lists for things we need in a spouse and things we find repulsive," he said.

"I don't think I used the word *repulsive*, but that's the idea," I replied with a chuckle.

"Well, whatever," he continued on. "The point is, I need help making up lists like that."

"What do you mean?" I asked. "Didn't I make it clear what to include?"

"No, no, you were clear. I guess *I'm* not clear. As you were talking, I realized my criteria up to this point have been . . . well, pretty basic."

I could hardly wait to learn what his criteria were. "Okay, so let's hear them."

"Well, just three points," he said. "First, she has to be good-looking . . . That should be on the list, right?"

"Many people find physical attraction important; so, yes, that's fine."

"Good. Second, we have to get along well—you know, laugh at the same things, talk easily, have fun together."

He seemed to wait for my assent, so I nodded and told him to keep going.

"And third, she has to love UCLA. I'm a *big* Bruin fan, and I go to all the games."

I waited several seconds for him to continue, but that was the extent of his list.

"I told you it's pretty basic," he said sheepishly.

"Is there nothing more you look for in a woman?" I asked.

He thought for a moment. "I suppose so. I've just

never written them out. So I'm looking for some help to get me started—you know, to get my wheels spinning."

"You're in luck," I said. "During this afternoon's session, I'm going to give the twenty-five most popular items on other singles' lists." The fellow looked eager, as if I were going to hand over a homework assignment for him to copy. "But understand, you've got to create your own list. That's the whole point of this exercise. I can't tell you what you want in a spouse. *You* have to decide."

So later that day, I shared with my audience—including the Bruin fan, who was ready with pen and paper—the twenty-five most popular must-haves. Here they are:

1. EMOTIONAL HEALTH

Most of the singles I talk to say they need a partner who is emotionally healthy. I affirm that wholeheartedly. After thirty years of experience in clinical psychology, I am convinced that no quality is as important to the eventual success of a marital relationship as the emotional health of both partners. As a matter of fact, I regularly state that no marriage can ever be stronger than the emotional health of the least healthy partner. If the person you're dating is self-absorbed, paranoid, overly defensive, or anything else that signals an emotional health deficit, watch out!

2. STRONG CHARACTER

A person whose character is strong tells the truth. More than just *telling* the truth, they *do* the truth and even *are* the truth. What I mean is that when they tell you something, you can rely on its being true. When they tell you they'll do something, they do it. And when they seem to be a certain way, they actually are that way over time. They are all about truth, and thus you can totally trust them.

3. ENERGY LEVEL

There are two things about energy that are equally crucial. First, a person's energy level is often a good indication of his emotional and physical health. There is something wrong with us when our energy is low. It almost always indicates some kind of internal problem that needs to be corrected. Too much energy also indicates a problem. People who are constantly on the go and seem unable to contain their energy probably need some kind of intervention.

Second, a person needs to have a *level* of energy similar to your own. Otherwise there are likely to be a lot of issues to contend with. Imagine the tension if a woman wants to be active all the time—going here and there, doing this and that—while her husband is a leisurely, low-energy type who likes to swing in the hammock and take an afternoon nap. Or if a man bounces out of bed in the morning, completing half his to-do list before 7:00 A.M., while his wife snoozes till 10:00, this is a mismatch that's bound to cause problems.

4. INTELLIGENCE

For a marriage to be strong and solid, two people need to be close in level of intelligence. Actual IQ has little to do with the success or failure of marriages. It is the *match* of two people's intelligences that is crucial. In my own clinical practice, I have noted that some persons are uneducated but highly intelligent; other persons have advanced degrees but often seem less intelligent in certain areas.

What's more, there are different types of intelligence. Some people learn a language far more rapidly than others, or maybe they can put a motor together faster, or even master new computer software in a snap. The type and amount of intelligence that is important to you need to be understood and delineated.

5. CHEMISTRY

Almost everyone wants to feel deeply "in love" with the person they marry. They want to feel what Romeo and Juliet felt when they first saw each other across the room. In short, they want to feel wild and passionate emotions exploding within them.

Chemistry is critical in romance, and romance is vital to the bonding that needs to take place for two partners. In fact, I often tell singles that when a man and woman have a lot in common but lack chemistry or "magic," they shouldn't try to force their friendship into a romance. Building a great marriage is virtually impossible without the attraction and excitement that come with passionate love.

6. FINANCIAL SECURITY

Some men have the misconception that all women are looking for a man who's rich. Judging from the thousands of single women I've talked with over the years, I don't think that's true. What the majority of women want is a spouse who will be *responsible to provide* for the family. In this regard, financial security—at whatever level—is important and does frequently show up on must-have lists.

The fact is, if a woman dreams of being home with the children during their growing-up years and is willing to forgo her own career plans until later in her life, then she needs a man who can earn a good living and provide a stable financial environment.

This, of course, is not totally a one-gender issue. Some men want to marry a woman who will work outside the home, provide additional finances for the family, and generally make a higher standard of living possible.

The matter of financial security is hotly debated in our society, but you need to decide whether it will be an item on your list.

7. VERBAL INTIMACY

This quality is more often mentioned by women, but nearly everyone would agree that a good marriage needs a lot of deep communication.

In several of my books, I have taken the position that men are seldom trained to communicate well when they are young boys. Our society tends to keep boys focused outside themselves. We teach them how to hit a ball with a bat and how to throw a football with a spiral. When it comes to communicating from deep within themselves, most boys simply aren't very good at it. They don't know how to access their deepest feelings and meanings, and apart from these, they are horribly inadequate in most communicative situations.

If the ability to communicate is crucial to you, get it on your list. For some persons, I would expect it to be the most important must-have of all.

8. CONFLICT-RESOLUTION SKILLS

Every marriage has conflict. Disagreements are the consequence of two unique persons expressing themselves on an unending number of issues. In great marriages, two people learn how to manage their conflicts thoroughly and efficiently so that harmony prevails most of the time. Marriages begin to fall apart when conflicts occur and seldom, if ever, get resolved.

9. PERSONAL HABITS

There are dozens of personal habits that may be critical to you, but I want to mention five in particular that singles have pointed out to me over and over.

First, *personal hygiene*. This includes the cleanliness of your body, hair, nails, and teeth.

Second, *punctuality.* How important is it to you that a person be on time, that he or she meets you when they say they will?

Third, *dependability.* If a person promises you something, does it shatter you if he or she simply doesn't "deliver"?

Fourth, *remembering important dates.* If your lover forgot your anniversary, your birthday, or any other special date, would that matter a lot to you?

Fifth, *orderliness.* Do you like a clean car, a clean apartment, a clean closet, and a clean office?

Whatever you would put on this list, it's likely that some personal habits are important to you.

10. SPIRITUALITY

For a lot of people I know, a deep commitment to spirituality is at the top of the list. If you think of your relationship with God as the most important thing in your life, it is undoubtedly crucial that you marry someone who has a similar view. If you have spent years deepening your prayer life, learning about spiritual disciplines, and practicing your faith, you would likely feel distant from someone who felt and acted differently.

11. SHARED INTERESTS

If you have five or six major interests, it's a good idea to find someone who shares two or three of them. Let's say you are passionate about travel, golf, biking, reading, classical music, and entertaining. It will be important to the success of your marriage to find someone who enjoys at least half of these activities.

Imagine getting married to someone who had none of these interests. For instance, what if your partner's major interests were stock car races, nightly partying, country music, boxing, gambling, and water sports? The two of you would be lucky to catch sight of each other every few days—and even when you did, you wouldn't have much to talk about.

12. SIMILAR POLITICAL AND SOCIAL VIEWS

If you and your lover hold extremely different views on politics and social issues, you're likely to experience tension and disharmony. If one of you is highly liberal and the other is very conservative, your conversations will probably be replete with statements such as "I can't believe you think that way!" or "How in the world can you support that?"

For some people, this item matters enormously. If it matters a lot to you, make sure to place it high on your must-have list.

13. INTEREST IN PARENTING AND APPARENT ABILITY TO DO IT WELL

If you have always wanted to have children and this is a major part of your life dream, then you should have this item on your list. Don't take it for granted! Some people simply do not want to have children, and even more important, some people have little apparent ability to participate fully in the parenting task. Others, of course, are just the opposite. They are drawn to parenting as they are drawn to nothing else, and they show great parenting promise.

14. PERSONALITY

Personalities come in a lot of different forms. For instance, here are some of the qualities I like very much about Marylyn's personality: her positive outlook on life, her willingness to both listen and talk, her range of assertiveness and reserve, her quiet strength, her low level of anger, her determination, her cheerfulness, her gratitude, her family bondedness, and her tireless efforts on behalf of those she loves.

I'm not sure that all of these qualities are totally within the category of personality, but this I do know: We all look for a person who has "ways of being" that we like and can live well with. What type of personality do you want in the person you marry?

15. VALUES

Values refers to principles that guide the way we live and make decisions. For instance, if one person believes that family is the most important group of all, then this person will want to distribute assets to the family, work for the family's welfare, and spend more time with the family than with any group or activity outside the family. And if the marriage partner does not share this value, there will be regular conflicts.

Other values include total honesty, generosity, community activities, environmental protection, animal rights, protection of the unborn, and freedom from governmental intrusion. There are dozens of possible values, and if you hold one or all of them with great passion, you may well want to put "values" at a high place on your list.

16. SKILLS

If you are a man, how important is it that your wife know how to cook, sew, shop, and clean as your mother always did? And if you are a woman, how much do you need a man who is handy around the house, who knows how to paint, do minor electrical work, and can fix a furnace in the middle of the night?

Whether you are a man or a woman, do you need someone who has athletic skill, such as snow skiing or waterskiing, golf or tennis skill, and who can dance and socialize well?

Some people have a lot more ability than others do. Which skills are important to you?

17. AMBITION

If your ambition is strong, it might be difficult for you to marry a person who is laid-back and unconcerned about career advancement or getting ahead. Think long and hard about this one. I have watched couples with differing levels of ambition, and I have seen how this distinguishing characteristic can cause a lot of discord. How ambitious are you to get ahead? And how important is it for you to marry someone who shares your ambition?

18. AGE

When Marylyn and I got married, age was a significant factor. The man was always supposed to be older, and the difference should be one to three years.

Our society has changed, and now the age variable has become much more elastic. The older a person becomes, the more likely he or she is to marry someone several years older or younger. And it is not at all uncommon for the woman to be older than the man.

Is age a critical variable for you? How do you think about it? Within what ages do you want your marital partner to be? Is it important enough to make your top ten list?

19. RACE

Some people would not think of marrying outside their race. For others, this issue doesn't matter one bit. What about you? We do know that divorce rates are higher for interracial marriages—not because of skin color or facial features, but because of cultural differences. But is this an item that should be in your top ten must-haves?

20. RELIGIOUS AFFILIATION

For many people, the boundary between Catholic and Protestant is becoming thinner, but would you cross that boundary in selecting a marriage partner? How about the boundary between Jewish and Christian, or between Christian and Buddhist?

Interreligious marriages have a higher divorce rate, too, but the question pertains directly to you: Is this a crucial issue in *your* eyes?

21. EDUCATION

A highly educated man told me recently that he used to think the person he married did not have to be college educated; she only needed to be intelligent. But over time, his thinking shifted, and he has concluded that he needs to marry someone who has finished college. He has found that this amount of formal education, and all that usually comes with it, is a requirement for him.

Other people in our society don't like what education does to a person, and they want no part of it in the man

or woman they choose to marry. As far as they are concerned, education imposes qualities and standards on a
person, and it makes some persons far less able to be
authentically themselves.

What about you? Do you want someone with the
same amount of formal education as you—or could you
not care less?

22. SEXUAL HISTORY

For many people, how their potential mate has han-
dled sexuality in prior relationships is important. Some
persons are extremely concerned that their mate be
"pure" in this area. Others tell me that they want to make
sure their mate is mature and experienced as a potential
sex partner. How do you feel about this issue?

23. HEIGHT AND BODY SHAPE

I have left three of our twenty-five spots for matters
relating to appearance. Since our society places so much
emphasis on looks, I am wondering how many of these
will make it onto your list of must-haves.

The first of these three is height and body shape. Some
tall women want a man who's taller than they are, and

that limits their pool of marriage candidates. And a six-foot-four-inch man may not feel comfortable with a woman who stands five-feet-one. Within what height range does the person of your dreams need to fall?

What about body shape? If you are a man, do you prefer a buxom woman? What about someone more diminutive? If you are a woman, does your man need to be trim and athletic—"tall, dark, and handsome"? Or would it be okay if he were a bit paunchy and over-weight?

24. FACIAL FEATURES

How important is a good-looking face to you? If you wouldn't describe another person as handsome or pretty, would you still be interested? Are facial features the important factor for you? If a person had great facial features, could you handle their being less than ideal in terms of height and weight?

25. CLOTHES STYLE

Is fashionable clothing important to you? Would it bother you if your spouse always wore clothes ten years out of style? Do you like a person significantly better if their clothes match, if they are well pressed and clean, and if they are well made and nicely tailored? How crucial is this for you?

RULES FOR FORMULATING YOUR MUST-HAVE LIST

First, you need to decide which ten of these twenty-five dimensions are most important to you (of course, you may include some that aren't on this list). I assume this entire task will not be easy. If it is, you might try being a little skeptical. To further clarify your thinking, try to arrange your ten must-haves from the most important to the least important. Then go back over your list to make sure that every item on your list is indeed an absolute, unequivocal must-have. If it's not, take it off your list.

If you get this list perfected so that it represents the person you must have to experience deep fulfillment in your life, you will have taken a giant step forward. This will be your "shopping list," and you should make sure that it is never far from you until the day you march down the aisle and say, "I do!"

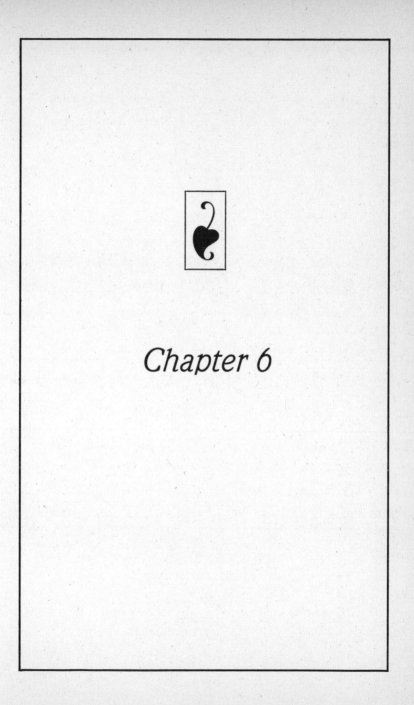

Chapter 6

THE TWENTY-FIVE
MOST PREVALENT
CAN'T-STANDS

Virtually every person is turned off by some qualities or habits in members of the opposite sex. The key is to figure out ahead of time which qualities these are for you. Once you have them figured out and written down, you can watch for them in every new person you date. Should you encounter one of these qualities during the early phases of dating someone, you can make a hasty and dignified exit from the relationship.

These disagreeable characteristics are what I refer to as "veto items." They are attributes of another person to which you respond so negatively that you wouldn't choose to spend the rest of your life with the person. In fact, regardless of how many positive qualities the man or woman may have, the presence of one of these unpleasant traits will determine your final decision all by itself.

CAN NEGATIVE QUALITIES CHANGE?

I am regularly asked if negative qualities are permanent. "Dr. Warren," someone may say, "just because a person has this quality now doesn't mean he'll always have it, does it?" Because I like to believe the best about everyone, my empathy always tempts me to give a positive reply, to assure the questioner that there is hope.

But after all these years of being a psychologist, I must tell you that offensive qualities tend to become ingrained in people's lives. Take any kind of addiction, for instance. These are usually learned behaviors that are extremely difficult to change. If you have a strongly negative response to such an addiction, and if the dating relationship is relatively new, you should be realistic about the possibility of the addiction "going away."

At the very least, you should certainly wait until the person brings the addiction under total control before you consider continuing the relationship. Otherwise, you risk living with someone for the rest of your life who has this can't-stand quality.

BUILD YOUR CAN'T-STAND
LIST THOUGHTFULLY

What are the qualities that you can't stand in another person—especially in a person with whom you expect to spend every day until you die? To help you build your list, I want to share what others have told me about their can't-stand items. See how you respond to each of these.

For reasons I discussed earlier, I want you to limit your list to ten items. I realize that you could probably rattle off fifty or a hundred things people do to aggravate you, but if you include all of them on your list, you may never find someone who meets your expectations.

1. LYING

If you notice your date lying to a restaurant server, a gas station attendant, a policeman, or anyone else, watch out! A person who will lie to a policeman will eventually lie to you. And if there is anything that most people can't stand in their most intimate relationship, it's lying. Deceitfulness breaks trust, and without trust there can be no intimacy. Without intimacy, a marriage loses its vitality at an early point.

Have you ever had a person lie to you? How did you

react? Do you feel strongly enough to make this one of your ten can't-stand items?

2. CHEATING

If you become aware that a person you are dating is a cheater, would you run in the other direction? I hope so, because any person who would do this may well be incapable of forming a deep and committed relationship with you. That's because cheating is almost always rooted in selfishness. It represents the behavior of people whose self-satisfaction is primary, whose sensitivity and empathy for you are far surpassed by their desire to gratify themselves.

If you encounter a man or woman who cheats, however smooth and charming the person may be, you should expect a thousand excuses and rationalizations to dismiss the action. These have often been practiced over time, and sometimes they are almost believable.

3. DOMINATING

Some people feel the need to dominate others. They try to take control of every situation, get you to do what they want to do, and give as little as they can to get everything they want. The behavior may be subtle or overt, but the feeling of being bullied is undeniable.

Imagine living for the rest of your life with one of these persons! If you find yourself thinking that it might be okay to have someone take charge of your life, be very cautious. Domineering and controlling behavior tends to become more and more habituated over time, and before you know it, you could be a slave to the person's wishes.

4. FINANCIAL IRRESPONSIBILITY

If you recognize that a person is financially irresponsible, what do you feel? If you imagine yourself being his or her financial partner for the rest of your life, could you live with continual overspending, lack of discipline, and disregard for budgets and boundaries? Some people have never been taught healthy financial principles. Others know what is right and wrong, but they have little control over their impulses.

This item always gets a lot of takers. Does it strike you as something you just couldn't tolerate in your marriage?

5. ANGER MISMANAGEMENT

If someone yells at other people when they are angry—even if these other people are "loved ones"—this is several steps worse than just feeling angry inside. And, of course, there are behaviors worse than yelling, such as

throwing things, striking with a fist or foot, driving reck-
lessly, or hurling all kinds of cusswords and verbal abuse
at another person.

Most of us can't stand to be around people who are
unable to control their anger. Would you be willing to put
up with a spouse who had an anger problem—or would
this item make your top ten can't-stand list?

6. PORNOGRAPHY

The habit of viewing pornography undermines every
good relationship. How do you feel about it? If you discovered that a person you are dating enjoys pornography,
would you have a strong negative response? If so, is it
among the top ten things you wouldn't want to live with
for a lifetime?

7. EXCESSIVE DRINKING OR DRUG USE

The consumption of alcohol and the use of drugs are
major activities in our society. How do you feel about
alcohol consumption by the person you will one day
marry? If you don't object to drinking *per se*, then how
much do you consider *too much*? What are your own limits, and what are your limits for the person you date?
What about someone who uses drugs?

8. SMOKING

Hundreds of thousands of people in our society smoke. Indeed, smoking is big business! But are you willing to put up with this "business" in your household—for a lifetime? Are you totally opposed to smoking, or does it not really concern you?

Through my research and seminars, I've discovered that smoking is one of the most frequently mentioned can't-stand items. Does it make your list?

9. GAMBLING

Gambling seems to be gaining a larger and larger foothold in America today. Some singles are troubled by the moral implications of gambling, others fear that gambling could develop into an addiction, and still others don't like to "throw money away" on this activity. How do you feel about it? If the person you date showed a lot of interest in gambling, would you object?

10. SEXUAL OBSESSIVENESS

Some men and women focus a lot of conscious attention on sexual matters. They think about sex and mention it regularly, allowing it to surface far more often than seems appropriate. If you meet a person who talks excessively about sex, does it make you uncomfortable? Does it bother you enough to make your top-ten list?

11. SLOPPINESS

If a person you date is sloppy, what response will you have? Suppose your date showed up with wrinkled clothes, a shirt half tucked in, and uncombed hair. Or let's say you hop into his or her car, and you have to move trash out of the way. What if you went to the person's apartment and discovered stacks of papers everywhere and dishes piled up in the kitchen. Would this bother you?

12. LAZINESS

Laziness is akin to sloppiness, but it's a little different. Sloppy people may not be lazy at all; maybe they're so busy accomplishing important things that they just can't be bothered by neatness and orderliness. Likewise, lazy people may not be very sloppy. They may have enough gumption to keep their car and apartment clean—but can't seem to muster the energy for anything else.

13. PROCRASTINATION

Do you think there's a place between laziness and sloppiness for procrastination? I do. If you've ever been a procrastinator, or roomed with one, you know the torment of putting things off. "I'll for sure get it done tomorrow," the well-intentioned procrastinator often says—and he means it. He definitely means it this time! But procrastination tends to become highly habituated, and when it does, frustration mounts for everyone involved. Is it a bothersome quality to you?

14. GOSSIPING

If you share personal and intimate information with someone, you don't want it spread around. But some people seem simply incapable of keeping their mouths shut. They're the ones who say things like, "I probably shouldn't tell you this, but did you know that Jane Smith has been married three times? She doesn't want anyone to know, so keep it to yourself." Does this kind of gossip bother you? Would it be hard to spend the rest of your life with someone you can't rely on to keep a secret?

15. Inappropriate Behavior

Have you noticed that some people frequently behave inappropriately? They talk too loud at social gatherings, make rude comments, laugh at odd times, tell offensive jokes, and maybe even embarrass their friends. Does this kind of inappropriateness concern you?

16. Penny-Pinching

I'm not talking here about people who are frugal—I'm referring to those who are so tightfisted they offend others. These are the people who don't offer to pay for anything—or manage to pay less than their share—when the restaurant check arrives. Or they always happen to be "short of cash" and let you pick up the tab. I feel taken advantage of by people like this. It seems to me that this kind of behavior emerges from a selfish and self-centered attitude. This is a quality I have a lot of trouble with. Do you?

17. "Foul" Talk

Some people throw a cussword into nearly every sentence. For whatever reason, they can't make a strong point without an expletive. When that happens in your presence, what is your feeling? If you assumed that this person was never going to change, would you end the relationship? Does it bother you much?

18. DEPENDENT ON OTHERS

If you notice that the person you're dating looks to Mom for a lot of answers to ordinary life questions, you can't assume that will stop if you get married. Or if the individual spends too much time with a group of immature friends, always needing to check with them before making plans with you, how would you feel? Does your reaction depend on how much you end up liking the person's mother or friends, or do you automatically assume there is something immature and undeveloped about this kind of dependence? If you catch a scent of it, do you want to run?

19. ARROGANCE

If the person you're dating is cocky and conceited, would you find it hard to tolerate? Let's say the man or woman has some social skills, but you detect an underlying attitude of haughtiness. It's as if the person says (verbally or nonverbally), "I'm always right, and I know better than you!"

In the name of confidence, some people are just *too* confident. And the question for you is, Do you find this behavior offensive enough to put it on your top ten list?

20. EXTREME SHYNESS

If you have dated people whose shyness kept them from talking much, led them to reveal almost nothing about themselves, and created a lot of nervousness around you and others, then you know how painful and awkward this quality can be.

I offer tapes to help singles with many different issues, and the one on managing shyness is consistently a top seller. It is a huge problem for a lot of people. But the only thing that matters right now is this: Do you have trouble relating to an extremely shy person, and is the problem significant enough for you to end a relationship?

21. DIFFERING MUSIC PREFERENCES

If your date plays a steady stream of classical music, and if classical music is of little interest to you, is that a big problem? Or if you like classical and your date thrives on rock 'n' roll, would you want to scream? If you want to scream, I assume you would have difficulty dealing with this difference over a long period of time.

22. SPIRITUAL INTOLERANCE

If you dated a person who espoused a spiritual position different from yours, would you respond negatively? What if the man or woman was intolerant of your views, always trying to persuade you to change? Does it bother you to be told that "you have to change" or else? Does it make you nervous about future differences?

23. "POLITICAL CORRECTNESS"

There is a lot of talk these days about being "politically correct." Typically, it centers on gender, race, sexual preference, and religious affiliation. How do you feel about it? Would you hate living with someone who criticized you for your lack of correctness? Or how would you like living with someone you thought of as "insensitive to social appropriateness"?

24. RECKLESS DRIVING

If a person's driving style is characterized as "too fast" and "too reckless" by you—even after you comment on it two or three times—would this constitute a veto item? Imagine feeling that you were risking your life every time you got in a car with this person. Could you live happily with someone who, in your mind at least, regularly threatened your well-being on the road?

25. FANATICISM

Could you ever be married to a fanatic—someone who gets charged up over politics or baseball or religious issues or environmental protection or whatever? Would it make a difference if you shared the same point of view, just to a lesser degree?

SELECT YOUR TOP TEN CAN'T-STAND ITEMS

Your challenge now is to select ten items for your can't-stand list, either from the ones I've mentioned or your own. Make sure that every one of them is so crucial to you that, if you encountered it in a person you dated, it would spell the end of the relationship. What the presence of any of these items would mean is that you wouldn't want to invest any more time, effort, or caring in this relationship. To further clarify your thinking, you may want to rank your ten items in order of offensiveness to you.

Now that you have both your must-have and can't-stand lists, you are ready to proceed down the dating trail. You know exactly what you are looking for—and exactly what you won't accept.

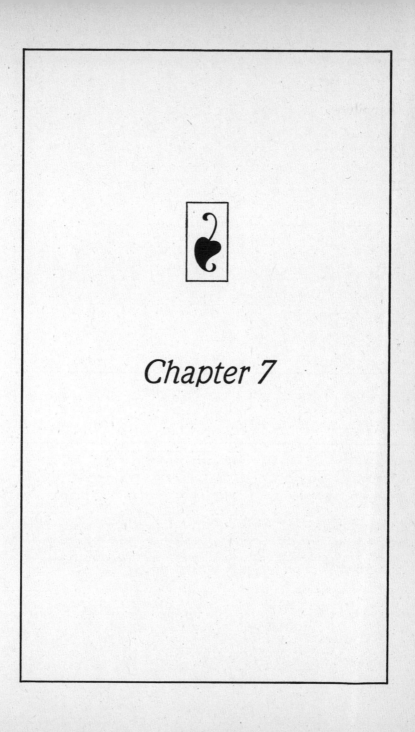

Chapter 7

THE POWERFUL IMPACT
OF EMOTIONAL HEALTH

I don't have an exact count, but I'm sure that I've counseled several thousand marital partners. Some of them came to me for help in working through relatively minor issues, but the majority of them were somewhere between hurting and hopeless. Marriages that had been dreamlike in the beginning had turned nightmarish, and in many cases, there were real doubts about their ability to survive. I wasn't always the "last stop" on the way to the divorce lawyer, but frequently I was.

I should tell you that fifteen or twenty years ago, I suddenly recognized something that had eluded me during the early years of my practice. In my frantic attempts to help people keep their marriages together, I had overlooked the most salient truth of all: Most of these people didn't have a "marriage" problem. That is, one or both partners had emotional difficulties, and when those individuals brought their personal problems into the relationship, the marriage went sour.

In 75 to 80 percent of all marriages that eventually end in divorce or separation, at least one of the partners suffers from an emotional health deficiency. Usually, this problem has haunted them for years, long before they got married. And if it doesn't get fixed, their marriage won't get well! I'm so convinced of this that I tell people that no marriage can ever be healthier than the emotional health of the least healthy partner. Individuals have to get healthy for marriages to improve.

You might say, "Yeah, but isn't everyone a little emotionally unhealthy?" My answer is a resounding, "NO!" Granted, there is an enormous amount of pain in our society, and broken families are the source of much of it. What's more, many people are confused about themselves and the direction of their lives. In fact, I can go even further and say that many persons are so wounded emotionally that they need to do a lot of work before they even think of getting married.

Still, the picture isn't completely bleak, because there are significant numbers of emotionally well people in our society. And here's the most crucial point I have to make in this chapter: Until you are one of these emotionally well persons, and until you fall in love with another emotionally well person, you aren't ready to be married.

WHAT DETERMINES EMOTIONAL HEALTH?

In my opinion, emotional health begins with a well-constructed self-concept. This means knowing yourself well, being well defined, and feeling good about yourself. Any person who suffers from a self-concept that has been poorly developed over time will usually show signs of an emotional health deficiency, which may be something as mild as low self-esteem expressed in the form of unnatural shyness and quietness, or something as overpowering as an explosive anger problem.

I watch communication patterns for signs of a well-developed or poorly developed self-concept. For instance, when I talk with someone who is healthy, our conversation has a natural flow to it. We take turns talking and listening, and there is a good pace to our dialogue. The conversation progresses smoothly because we both listen carefully to each other's points, and we respond to them. We each stay on the subject and respect what the other is saying.

On the other hand, when I encounter people who

have a hard time looking me in the eye while they talk to me, I begin to wonder what's going on within them. If they never initiate conversation, if they seldom respond to my comments, or if there is little indication that they are following the general line of our discussion, I suspect they are experiencing the anxiety that almost always comes from a lack of self-confidence.

I reach the same conclusions if the other person won't stop talking. If you pursue the roots of this problem, you'll almost always find that the individuals aren't sure of their worth, so they try to compensate by controlling the conversation. This kind of defensive behavior keeps a relationship from flourishing. When communication is poor, the relationship is sure to suffer.

I don't immediately conclude that these people are incapable of a long-term relationship. What I do conclude is that their interpersonal skills are not yet well developed and that their ability to form a relationship is probably handicapped by their low self-esteem. If these problems continue even after the stress of the early dating stages has lessened, the relationship is bound to have some trouble.

Significant communication problems like these are a tip-off to other, possibly more serious, underlying emotional issues. The presence of these symptoms does not mean a relationship is doomed. But they sharpen my hearing, and I watch closely for other signs of an inadequately developed self-concept.

OTHER COMMUNICATION DIFFICULTIES

Almost everyone experiences some degree of nervousness on a first date. What you need to look for are more advanced signs of an emotional health deficiency. For instance, if during the first and maybe second dates there are continuing and significant communication problems with the other person, I would suspect that any developing relationship would be disappointing to both individuals. If your date continued to talk too much or too little, if he simply didn't show any listening skills, if he asked almost nothing about you, or if he moved the conversation abruptly in too many directions, this would clearly indicate significant problems. These would represent an important barrier to relational growth.

This brings up an even more important issue. Any person who is a healthy marriage candidate will express attitudes of unselfishness. There is simply no quality more central to the eventual love that will bind two people together than this one. If you notice that your date is completely selfish, showing almost total disregard for your wishes and opinions, you may be in the presence of a serious disorder—narcissism. These people have an inflated sense of self-importance, and they don't care much about others. As you can imagine, narcissists have a very difficult time communicating and building relationships.

CHARACTER DISORDERS

A person who suffers from a character disorder frequently has significant behavioral or emotional problems that will almost certainly spell disaster for any marital relationship.

One of the most difficult aspects of identifying people with character disorders is that they tend to be unusually charming. They often present themselves in an engaging, reassuring manner, and before long you may find yourself sharing your most tender and intimate feelings. Sometimes, they may be relatively unaware of their strategy. Obviously, you need to be attentive to anyone who begins a relationship in an overly charming way. And it may take you more than two dates to discover some of these elusive character disorders.

At the center of a character disorder is a poorly developed conscience. These persons behave out of their own desires and impulses, and they pay little attention to how their actions may affect you. As a matter of fact, if they can get their own perceived needs met, even if that means hurting you in some way, they will do so.

People with these kinds of disorders tend to lie, cheat, exaggerate, and take advantage of others. When a person lies to me early in a relationship—even telling "little white lies" or "shading the truth"—I immediately want to protect myself against further deception. I know that a person who lies once is almost sure to lie again. A person who manipulates me once is going to manipulate me again. Once a cheater, always a cheater unless some intervention changes the internal pattern. When you become involved with a liar, a manipulator, a cheater, someone who is irrational or rude or inconsiderate, or a person who takes advantage of you, back away immediately! The prognosis for this type of disorder (that is, the likelihood that it can be treated successfully) is low. You simply do not want to become involved with a person who has a character disorder.

Of course, this is not to say that any person who begins a relationship in a charming, friendly, and sensitive way is "one of those clever character disorder-type persons" who will eventually do you in. I am only suggesting that a marriage involving someone with a character disorder is almost surely doomed to failure. If you can detect this early on, you will save yourself from a tremendous amount of pain.

WHAT ABOUT NEUROSES?

A neurosis is an inner emotional state characterized by an attempt to manage excessive anxiety. Persons who suffer from neuroses generally are depressed, fearful, obsessive-compulsive, or overly anxious in response to certain cues from the environment. If you encounter a person who suffers from a neurosis, you may wish to delay a dating relationship with this person until he or she has a chance to work through the problem.

Neuroses, in my opinion, are far less indicative of long-term catastrophic marital relationships than are character disorders. But if you get involved with a person who has a neurosis, you may wish you hadn't gotten started with the relationship until the individual made progress in overcoming the problem through psychotherapy.

Consider depression, for instance. Apart from biochemical problems, depression is in the neurosis category. I have found that the three fundamental sources of depression are: anger turned on the self; guilt and shame; and an experience of loss. All of these causes of depression can be managed effectively in psychotherapy. But if they aren't, and if a person continues to be depressed over time, any primary relationship is bound to suffer. Every kind of neurosis can be effectively treated, but the time to do so is before any serious dating relationship begins.

ADDICTIONS

I have never seen a good marriage that involved one person who had an active and untreated addiction of any kind. The addiction usually whittles away at the quality of the marriage and, if not adequately treated, will lead to failure. That's why I encourage persons who are going out on dates to watch for behaviors that may indicate addictions. If your date seems too eager to "have a drink"—and then another and another—this may signal a problem. Or if the person wants to have a drink wherever you go, this may be a danger sign. There are some twenty-five million alcoholics in this country, but an even bigger issue is the problem drinkers who have not sought help for their disability.

I should hasten to mention that I have known many wonderful mates who were recovered alcoholics. Even though the term *alcoholic* is accurate for them over a lifetime, these people worked hard to recover and make a great contribution to their marriage. But without going through the difficult recovery process, alcoholics are highly dangerous if you are looking for a happy, long-term marriage.

There are other addictions to which you should be alert. A sexual addiction or an addiction to pornography or an eating disorder—any of these will nearly always spell defeat for a marital relationship unless they are treated. Gambling has become a larger and larger problem in this country. Compulsive shopping is a similar problem. When a person's self-esteem seems to require a constant accumulation of goods that they can't afford, you know that you have encountered a person with an addiction.

Other addictions are more difficult to identify. For instance, ambition is a marvelous quality in a future mate. But when ambition pushes a person to have an unbalanced work schedule, you may indeed be involved with a workaholic. Workaholism and great marital experiences are vicious opponents.

How Is Your Emotional Health?

Because emotional health so dramatically influences all of our relationships—especially marriage—we need to honestly assess our own degree of health. Consider these questions about yourself:

1. Am I emotionally healthy in relation to the categories we have discussed?

2. How well established is my self-concept?

3. How well do I know myself and like myself?

4. Am I totally free of character-disorder tendencies?

5. Do I have any untreated addictions?

6. Do I suffer from issues related to past physical or sexual abuse, which I have never worked through?

If you discover that you are not emotionally healthy in some way, get about the task of improving in that area. Do this before you begin another dating relationship. Take some time off from dating to address this part of your life! Dating usually leads to more dating, and more dating often leads to a serious relationship. You need to get yourself healthy before you get yourself into any serious dating relationship.

EMOTIONAL HEALTH BEGINS WITH UNCONDITIONAL LOVE

In order to be emotionally healthy, you and any person you date must become authentic. That is, you can never be healthy and content until you feel free to be that person you truly are at your center. This kind of emotional health requires that you make authentic decisions from moment to moment—decisions about large and small matters in your life. By making wise, thoughtful decisions, you effectively identify your true self, especially if you make the decisions from deep within yourself and only after you have taken into consideration all relevant data. This decision-making process requires that you be free to live your life without the drive to please any other man or woman. For this to be the case, you need to have a radical experience with unconditional love.

There are many ideas about the ultimate source of this kind of love, but I should tell you that my own belief is that it comes from the one true God. It is when you get into a right relationship with this God that you are set free to become the person you truly are—your authentic self.

What you want to find is a person who has experienced this kind of life-defining experience. If the person you encounter has experienced true unconditional love, and if he or she has worked hard to make authentic decisions about every aspect of life, I guarantee that you've found an emotionally healthy person. (For further information on this subject, see my book *Finding Contentment: When Momentary Happiness Just Isn't Enough*.)

CHARACTERISTICS OF AN EMOTIONALLY HEALTHY PERSON

We have talked a lot about signs of emotional health problems. Now I want to briefly mention three qualities that indicate emotional health. The first is generosity. Generous people give freely of themselves—the things they have, their time, their energy, and their feelings.

The second is truthfulness. Someone who tells the truth is at least on his way to emotional health. So important is truthfulness that I often say that at the very core of emotional health is a deep and passionate commitment to the truth.

The third is kindness. In seventeen cross-cultural studies of what people are looking for in a marital partner, kindness was in the top two in every study. We all want to be around people who are kind, because we sense that kindness comes out of an inner place that is healthy.

I'll leave you with this encouragement: If you find a person who is emotionally healthy, you will have eliminated 75 to 80 percent of the causes of divorce. You should spend more time with this kind of person, especially if you find all the rest of your must-haves and none of your can't-stands.

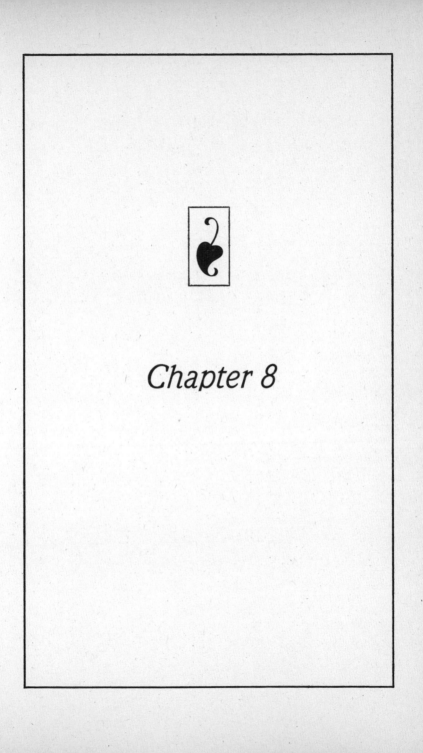

Chapter 8

DIFFERENCES THAT YOU MUST NOT OVERLOOK

If you want to make an accurate decision about whether or not you should continue dating a person—and if you want to make it within two dates—pay close attention to how much the two of you are alike. Once you're convinced that someone matches up well with your must-have and can't-stand lists, you will benefit enormously from your careful observance of one other principle: Find somebody to love who is a lot like you. This principle is well documented by empirical research, and I have come to believe in it with a lot of confidence.

After I wrote the book *Finding the Love of Your Life*, I was invited to appear on many radio and television programs. The one question I was asked on nearly every program was: "Is it really true that two people who have many similarities have the best chance of making their marriage work?" And my one-word answer every time was, "Definitely!"

In fact, similarities are so critical to a good marriage that I want to reemphasize their importance in this book. I also want to tell you about my new clinical findings that allow me to specify for you what I now consider to be the most critical similarities of all.

You may be thinking, *We hear so much about opposites attracting. Doesn't that happen?* It is true that opposites often attract. It's also true that they usually drive each other crazy over the long haul. In my observation of several thousand couples, I can tell you that the greater the differences between two people, the greater the drain on their marital energy. So strongly do I believe this that I have repeated over and over my admonition: "For couples, similarities are like money in the bank, and differences are like debts they owe." Every difference requires an enormous amount of hard work to manage, and this subtracts from the energy needed to keep a marriage thriving.

THE DIFFICULTY OF FINDING SOMEONE SIMILAR TO YOU

I don't discount how hard it is to find someone who is a lot like you. It has always been difficult, and it's become even more so since the days when your parents were considering marriage.

The key statistic in this regard involves the movement in America from rural to urban areas. Just after World War II in the United States, one out of every three persons lived on a farm. But by 1979, just thirty years later, only one family in twenty-eight lived on a farm. The migration within the forty-eight states was astounding as people moved into cities from rural areas. People were suddenly living next door to other people whose traditions and customs were significantly different. Communities became composed of many races that had never before been mixed. It was more than just racial diversity; it involved the mixing of persons from many areas of the country who had dissimilar traditions and customs. This is no doubt a significant reason why the divorce rate tripled in the United States between 1950 and 1980.

All kinds of research studies have shone a spotlight on the risks inherent in marrying someone very different from you. J. Phillippe Rushton, a professor at the University of Western Ontario in Canada, summarized a considerable body of research: "Several studies have shown that not only the occurrence of relationships but also their degree of happiness and stability can be predicted by the degree of matching of personal attributes."

In one study, a team of researchers administered a psychological test to three groups, each consisting of thirty-five couples. The first group included couples who were happily married, the second group consisted of couples having trouble but planning to stay together, and the final group contained couples on the verge of separation. The happy couples were significantly similar in general activity, friendliness, and personal relations. Unhappy couples tended to be dissimilar. Both groups of unhappy couples were significantly dissimilar on emotional stability.

Finally, after a careful review of the literature, researchers White and Hatcher concluded: "Clinical studies available indicate that similarity is associated with marital success and is less associated with marital instability and divorce. Evidence suggests that dissimilarity per se is associated with marital instability and divorce."

THE IMPORTANCE OF SIMILARITY

I know a couple, Matt and Kristen, who have a lot in common. Because their families lived only a few houses apart when they were growing up, they actually knew each other from the third grade on, and they began going together when they were juniors in high school. They were both popular in school, about equally attractive, and they had a large number of mutual friends.

Their families were both upper-middle class, active in church, and they held strong religious beliefs. While the two families had met only occasionally, they were unusually similar. There was a shared commitment to the community and especially to the activities of the three children in each family.

Matt was an athlete and Kristen wasn't, but she had as much interest in sports as he did. She read the sports pages every day, knew all about the local sports teams, and the two of them discussed sports a lot. They listened to music, took long walks together, and talked and laughed. They were equally ambitious, similarly intelligent, liked the same shows and entertainment, both loved children, and their goals overlapped almost completely.

Following high school, they went off to college—different schools, rivals actually, but both in the same large city. They dated each other steadily, then broke off and dated others, then got back together—a pattern that continued until they were out of school. Kristen then went off with her family for a year in Europe; Matt stayed home but visited her for two or three weeks at the end of her stay there. That was when they seemed to know they wanted to be together permanently. While they waited for three or four years, they were "on track" and headed in the same direction. And they were finally married nearly ten years after their first date.

In a case like this, with so many similarities, you would think their chances of being successful in marriage would be very high. And you're right. If every couple had this much in common, the divorce rate in this country would be significantly lower. There just aren't all those differences to argue about that so many new couples have. And over the long haul, shared values and interests provide a stable environment for raising children and pursuing each partner's life goals.

Matt and Kristen were fortunate; because they came from homes with so much in common, dozens of expectations, practices, and customs were the same. It's as though these two started with a million dollars in the bank, and they owed almost nothing. They have a lifetime to enjoy their family, grow individually, and build something wonderful together.

SEVEN SIGNIFICANT SIMILARITIES

I have counseled hundreds of couples who were thinking about getting married, and I have kept track of many of them through the years. I have carefully noted their similarities and dissimilarities, and I've come to believe that certain key similarities contribute in an unusually profound way to marital success. I want to spell out for you the seven most crucial ones.

1. SPIRITUAL HARMONY

I have traveled back and forth across the United States, holding seminars for single persons as well as married couples. I have talked with hundreds of these people, and I have come to the conclusion that the most important similarity for any couple—whether or not they know it at the time—concerns spirituality.

I am not referring here to shared "religious affiliation," although this is sometimes important, too. I am referring to the deeper matter of spirituality, which has to do with the larger context within which you perceive your life to be lived. Fundamentally, the question revolves around your belief in and relationship with a God—and not just *a* God, but a personal God. If you believe that there is a God, that He can be related to personally, that He created you and cares deeply about you, then your life may well be significantly influenced by your interactions with Him.

If you are deeply spiritual and the person you think

about marrying has almost no spiritual interest, the two of you are bound to encounter a barrier that separates you. If you do, you will frequently experience a deep sense of frustration that borders on agony.

Spirituality relates to central life functioning. If one person has a major spiritual interest and strongly held beliefs, and the other person feels indifferent and dispassionate toward this area, trouble is sure to ensue.

But here is a paradoxical fact: Spirituality may not be a crucial similarity if neither partner has any spiritual interests—and never expects to have any. Interestingly, however, most couples who stay together over a long period of time do develop a more pressing spiritual curiosity. So spiritual interest is certainly worth considering; it definitely is if you have a keen spiritual interest now or think you may in the future.

2. DESIRE FOR VERBAL INTIMACY AND ABILITY TO BE INTIMATE

Intimacy has the potential for lifting you and your lover out of the lonely world of separateness and into the stratosphere of emotional oneness. But if two people have a significantly different level of desire for intimacy, the relationship will surely suffer. Moreover, even if their desire for intimacy is similar, the relationship can be painfully frustrating if one person knows how to foster intimacy and the other person doesn't.

Since intimacy for two people refers to the sharing of their deepest feelings, thoughts, dreams, fears, and yearnings, it requires that both people be able to do at least three things well. First, each person must be able to access these thoughts and feelings way down at the center of him- or herself. Second, having once located all of this sensitive material, the man or woman must be able to put it into words and be courageous enough to verbalize it to another person. Third, each person must be able to listen accurately and intently, thus making the other person feel understood and valued.

When two people have a mutual interest in developing intimacy and the ability to do so, they will automatically become bonded, fused, and merged with each other. They will literally interlace the most important inner parts of themselves. This leads them to become what the Bible calls "one flesh"—the sense that their identities overlap, that the two of them become as one.

3. LEVEL OF ENERGY

Some couples who get into trouble with each other come from very similar backgrounds and have highly similar values. But if they have energy levels that are dissimilar, they will suffer all the troubles experienced by people who are much less similar than they are.

If you date a person who seems lethargic, try to figure out what the problem is. There is always a physical or psychological reason for lethargy. If it's a biochemical cause, it needs to be treated—and long before you engage in a serious dating relationship with them. On the other hand, if you date someone who is manic—someone with so much energy they can hardly control themselves—the long-term consequences can be just as serious. A manic-depressive illness can be treated with medication, and it must be for a marriage to work. But perhaps even more important is the experience of dating someone who is neither "pathologically" up nor down, but whose energy is significantly more or less than yours. Treat this matter with great seriousness!

4. LEVEL OF AMBITION

Our society highlights every person's ambition. If you have little or none, it quickly becomes obvious. And if you have a lot, it will be just as apparent. Are you content to put in your forty-hour workweek, come home and unwind, and involve yourself in sports or gardening or a musical instrument? If you are, you need to marry someone who has the same amount of ambition.

But if you are a get-up-and-go kind of person, someone who wants to rise to the next career level as soon as you can, someone who is motivated by goals and lofty dreams for the future, you need to find someone with similar ambition.

I have seldom encountered two people with very different ambition levels who found living with each other anything other than painful.

5. EXPECTATIONS ABOUT ROLES

This means both partners have compatible ideas about their duties and responsibilities in the relationship and household. In this time of great change in men's and women's roles within a marriage, I have seen happy couples with a variety of viewpoints on this issue. I know a man who resigned from his executive position to take care of the kids and the home while his wife works full-time. They seem remarkably happy with their arrangement. On the other hand, a number of my friends seem to be moving toward an equal distribution of work. Both partners work almost the same number of hours outside the home, and they divide the household chores. They appear happy, too. And some of the couples I know are quite traditional—the wife takes care of the kids and the household while the husband earns a living for them.

The point is, if both people agree on the work distribution and roles they will fulfill, it doesn't matter which variation they choose. But if they don't agree, there's a big price to be paid!

6. INTERESTS

When there are several things two people enjoy doing together, they have a large field on which they can happily play the game of life. I have always held that it is best if these interests reach across categories. For instance, if all five of the couple's common interests are athletic, it will be less beneficial to the relationship than if the five are spread across music, sports, theater, reading, and travel.

If you date a new person, one of the first things you can find out is what their major interests are. You probably won't have trouble finding out this information, since most people love to talk about their hobbies and passions. If you find that two or three of the person's interests overlap with your own, that's a great start to a relationship. But if your interests don't overlap at all, the relationship doesn't have much of a chance.

7. PERSONAL HABITS

Most personal habits seem so trivial and inconsequential when you're dating. But when you get married and live with someone every day, these little habits become magnified. Here are some examples of habits that can create conflict: punctuality, cleanliness, orderliness, dependability, responsibility, and weight management. We could mention dozens of other habits each person needs to consider before committing to a lifelong relationship. Watch closely for habits that may grate on your nerves.

WHY I WROTE THIS CHAPTER

Frankly, I was afraid that you might fail to get some of these important similarities and dissimilarities on your must-have or can't-stand lists. They have a way of sneaking up on you. You don't notice how important they are until you are around them for a while and the discrepancy between you and the other person suddenly develops a painful volume you hadn't noticed before.

For instance, if one of you is unusually clean, and the other one isn't, and if you spend all your dating time in the "clean" environment, you might miss how problematic this could be for both of you. And if you spend too much dating time in activities that require you to "do" something, and if there isn't much time left over to talk at a deep level, you may not recognize what a different need you have to share your deepest thoughts and feelings.

Find somebody to love who is a lot like you, and it will be like money in the bank for your long-term relationship.

Chapter 9

THE PRINCIPLES OF
NEGOTIATING A
GREAT DEAL

Some years ago, I came to a conclusion about mate selection that sounds so pragmatic and unromantic that it almost embarrasses me to share it with you. It is this: When you are searching for a marriage partner, you can expect to attract a person whose total "set of attributes" is approximately equal to your own. This is the principle of the marketplace. You want to find the best person you can, but this best person will largely depend on what you bring in trade.

The fact is that all of us want to get a "good deal" when it comes to choosing a mate. A good deal in a marriage partner is defined as "a person who brings at least as many qualities to the marriage as you do." There is something about this principle that strikes me as a little crass. It sounds so businesslike—you give me *that*, and I'll give you *this*. But, over time, I have never encountered a successful marriage in which both people didn't think they had negotiated a good deal.

WHAT DO YOU HAVE TO OFFER?

Virtually everyone would agree that people bring differing sets of qualities to the mate-selection process. Some individuals are unusually intelligent, kind, mature, good-looking, physically fit, athletically gifted, musically talented, and spiritually thoughtful. They are what I call the "breezers," because attracting potential mates is a breeze for them. Persons of the opposite sex are eager to date them and even marry them. Other persons bring a more moderate set of qualities to the "negotiating table." And still others bring significantly fewer qualities. One of the first things you have to do before you go "shopping" for a marriage partner is to determine what you have to offer.

In order to speed this process, and to quantify it, I have developed what I call a "bottom-line" test, which I mentioned in an earlier chapter (this is part of my "Finding the Love of Your Life Kit"—information about this resource can be found at the end of the book). It consists of a hundred dimensions—or qualities—on which you rate yourself from 1 to 10. Then you total your score. The final number will fall somewhere between 100 (if you rate yourself only a 1 on each dimension) and 1,000 (if you rate yourself a 10 on each of the qualities).

Through my research and clinical practice, I have determined that it's best for persons to choose a mate whose bottom-line score is close to their own. In fact, my experience is that these scores need to fall within fifty to seventy-five points of each other for the two persons to feel that they negotiated a good deal.

WHICH QUALITIES ARE MOST IMPORTANT?

You know what I know: Society says that appearance is the most important quality of all. In fact, in some circles, if you bring exceptionally good looks to the "mate-selection market," you can win almost any person you encounter. Appearance is far and away the most sought-after quality today.

Of course, we should not forget that the divorce-separation rate in our country is well above 60 percent. If appearance is the quality usually identified as most important, then we should be extremely skeptical about its value because of this incredible failure rate. I strongly suspect that my mother was right when she said that beauty is only skin deep. There are many qualities more meaningful than appearance when it comes to selecting the right marriage partner.

So which qualities are most important for you? Hopefully you were able to determine this when you created your must-have and can't-stand lists. The truth is, the singles I meet all seem to have different lists. Their lists depend on who they are, the environment they grew up in, what they've learned from previous relationships, and what their goals are. Some need a mate who has a dynamic personality and social skills that make a great impression on everyone. Others need to marry someone with high intelligence. Still others require artistic interests, well-developed creative talents, or a keen wit. Under the best of circumstances, the most important qualities of a man and a woman will fulfill each other's most pressing needs.

THE IMPORTANCE OF THE BOTTOM-LINE SCORE

As blunt as it may sound, no one wants to marry someone "beneath" them. I'm not talking necessarily about social class, family status, wealth, or education. I'm talking about the *sum total* of qualities a person brings to marriage. Whether a man or woman primarily seeks someone with deep spirituality, high energy, sterling character, or the patience of Job, that individual fundamentally wants someone whose bottom-line score is similar to his or her own. And they *should* want this, because I have seldom known two spouses who were happy together who didn't have this kind of equality.

Obviously, then, before you go looking for a spouse, you need to make a careful appraisal of what you will take to the "negotiations." Because the last thing you want is to marry someone who brings a lot more to the relationship than you do—or a lot less.

The other day, a man named Ben stopped by my office to tell me about his inventory results. "Dr. Warren, I took your test, and I got a bottom-line score of 650. But here's the exciting part: My fiancée, Brittany, also took the test, and she got a bottom-line score of 825. Looks like I'm getting a pretty good deal, huh?"

It seemed that he had missed the entire point of this exercise. He was obviously thrilled to get the better end of the deal.

"To be honest with you, Ben, I don't think that's good news," I said.

His expression changed from animated to somber in a matter of seconds. "Well, why not?" he asked. "What man wouldn't want to marry a woman who has it all— even if we're not 'ideally matched,' as you say?"

"I'm not trying to be unkind," I said, "but think of it this way: If you marry Brittany, you might spend the rest of your life worrying about every man she meets. Once she realizes that you bring less to the relationship than she does, she's likely to feel as if she made a big mistake. And when she meets men who would score closer to her 825, she may well be attracted to them. You see, it's not about *you* getting a 'great deal'—it's about both you *and* your partner getting a great deal. To do that, you must be closely matched."

Naturally, Ben didn't like my answer. He looked as if he held a winning lottery ticket—only to be told it had expired. Nevertheless, I had to be truthful with him. I knew that he and Brittany were so unevenly matched that a marriage for them would spell big trouble.

SOME PEOPLE FEEL "SHORTCHANGED" IN THEIR MATE SELECTION

Some attractive men and women seem to get "offers" only from people who would score below them on the bottom-line inventory. These are people I refer to as "shortchanged." These are persons whose love-life motto is "no decent offers have been received." Most short-changed persons feel strongly that, for whatever reason, the mate-selection process has not treated them fairly. Somehow people in their range of qualities don't pay attention to them. Their virtues have been underestimated and their defects overestimated, so they manage to attract only those who seem inferior to them.

I know hundreds of persons in this group—both men and women—who move through life feeling cheated by the mate-selection process. These are the people who score, say, a 600 on the inventory of qualities, but garner interest from members of the opposite sex who score 450. It seems that these 450 people are trying to manipulate—even bilk—their way into a deal that isn't at all good for this oft-overlooked 600 person. What the shortchanged individual desperately wants is for one of the 600s to take notice. Why can't these 600 people make a few offers?

If you feel frustrated that no one of your caliber pays attention to you, there are at least three possible reasons for your plight. The first is that you are scoring yourself too highly, that your own bottom-line number is unrealistically inflated, and this miscalculation repeatedly makes you feel cheated and disregarded. Overestimation of one's bottom-line score occurs frequently, and the culprit is often a well-meaning parent who tried to help you believe in yourself, but actually convinced you of things about yourself that simply were not true.

The second reason that some people feel short-changed is that they have not learned to present themselves effectively. For instance, if they deserve to score high on the personality scale, but they are so quiet that no one can discover what they are like, they are sure to be undervalued. And if they have never learned to articulate their ideas and opinions, they are likely to be undervalued on intelligence. The same is true about appearance—when otherwise attractive people dress slovenly or do not keep themselves well groomed, they sell themselves short. If you feel undervalued by the opposite sex, ask yourself about the effectiveness of your presentation.

The final reason for feeling shortchanged is a complex one. It has to do with the matter of "value-weighting." For instance, if your primary strength is intelligence, and if you deserve a 10 on this dimension, it isn't wise to hang around people whose focus in life is parties and football games. Your 10 may get reduced to a 1 because this social group doesn't value it highly. The same is true of spirituality. If your spiritual life is critical to you, and if you have become a veritable spiritual giant, spending time with persons who think spirituality is strange may reduce the strength of your score. What matters most to the "judges" is crucial when it comes to their determining your bottom-line score. So the secret is to associate with people who highly value your primary qualities.

If you are one of the many singles who feel short-changed by the mate-selection process, you are no doubt desperate to correct this unfairness. You want to find the caliber of person you deserve. Remember this: The person you find will be the result of complex negotiations, and now that you have given some attention to the qualities you bring, I want to talk to you about the best ways to negotiate a great deal for yourself.

NEGOTIATING PRINCIPLE 1:
PRIORITIZE YOUR "SHOPPING LIST"

If you go shopping for groceries, and if you have exactly fifty dollars to spend, you probably won't be able to buy everything on your list. So you have to ask yourself which items are most important to you. You sift through your priorities: *I'll buy bread and skip potato chips. And I'll take the pound of ground beef but forgo the six-pack of soda.* Obviously, this is a critical part of the shopping process. Once you have prioritized your list, you are prepared to search for the items that you most need and want.

Something similar needs to happen when you are

shopping for a marriage partner. The first thing you must do is determine what you bring to the negotiations, your sum total of assets or your bottom-line score. This will inform you of how much you can afford—that is, how many attributes the person will have who will want to date you.

You will then know the bottom-line score of the person you can attract. This is like knowing how many dollars you have to spend at the grocery store. And now the fun begins. You get to determine *how* you want to spend this total amount. Surely you don't want to waste any of it on attributes that are not absolutely crucial to you.

So you begin to prioritize the virtues on your shopping list, ranking in order the qualities you seek. There are some critical secrets to take into consideration in this process. For instance, you may not want to spend too much of your budget on superficial items. I have noted that great marriages are nearly always built on attributes that are central to a person's character and personality. When you meet someone who has a truly lovely and charming personality, your estimate of his or her appearance may go way up— even if that person is only slightly above average in appearance. Some studies indicate that spouses who are deeply in love estimate their lover's appearance as significantly more attractive than does a jury of objective peers.

Herein lies a secret negotiating tool. Look for the qualities that are connected with the person's internal, deep-down being. These are the qualities that will endure, that will keep contributing to the richness of the marriage year in and year out. Instead of spending very much of your allotted amount on good looks and a sleek figure, spend generously on good character, unselfishness, and kindness.

Here's another secret I've discovered: You can get a bargain on these internal qualities. That is, you won't have to spend nearly as much as they're really worth. But when it comes to appearance, you will have to pay an enormous premium, and over time, you will inevitably be disappointed—especially if you had to shell out a big percentage of your budget. Like a new car that dramatically depreciates in value as soon as it's driven off the lot, physical appearance goes down in value far more rapidly than you might expect. But "soul qualities" grow in value every year for the rest of your life.

NEGOTIATING PRINCIPLE 2:
INVEST IN RAW MATERIALS

I talk to singles every chance I get about the importance of investing in *potential*. You often don't have to pay nearly as much for qualities that have not yet been actualized. If you develop an eye for high-quality potential, this may well help you obtain a wonderful deal.

Suppose a woman wants a man with great ability to provide financial security. In my opinion, there is nothing wrong with a woman wanting a man who can support a lifestyle that includes a family and a comfortable home. At least, there's nothing wrong with this unless she pays too much because she lets this quality dominate her thinking—or because she wants this security *right now*. If she can spot a man who has the raw materials for becoming a good provider—even if it's going to take years to develop—her cost will be substantially less.

For instance, I know a couple who were as poor as church mice when they married. The man had just returned from military service, and he hadn't gone on to graduate school. The wife agreed to teach school while he studied to be a lawyer. Eventually, he joined a law firm, jumped through all the usual hoops, and finally became a partner. Now this couple enjoy a comfortable lifestyle.

Maybe this selection on her part was obvious, but the principles remain the same when the choice is not so obvious: Look for a person who is ambitious, hardworking, determined, and reliable. Hitch your wagon to this kind of star, and the eventual prize will be exactly what you want.

The key is that you can get a much better deal if you can find a person who, over time, is likely to develop the very qualities you admire the most. Find the qualities you admire in a person when they are budding rather than when they are in full bloom.

Negotiating Principle 3:
Find a Person Whose Dreams for the Future Overlap with Your Own

Sadly, most persons who are shopping for a marriage partner fail to inquire thoroughly about the long-term aspirations of their prospective mates. Yet I have come to believe that most persons will move astoundingly in the direction of their dreams. If you find a person whose dreams are much like your own, you can often get a phenomenal bargain. Other suitors may overlook this critical dimension, and they may not be willing to pay nearly as much for dreams as they're really worth.

I know a man who dreamed as a child that he would one day work for the United Nations in a Third World country. He longed to serve this way, and, besides, he wanted to see the world and experience the richness of living in another culture. The woman he eventually married had similar dreams as a young person. When they discovered that their aspirations overlapped, they decided to marry. And together, they made their dream come true. They moved to Africa, served in the United Nations, and grew by leaps and bounds as a couple in a foreign land. They are incredibly glad they became marriage partners because they helped each other realize their dreams.

In my book *Learning to Live with the Love of Your Life . . . and Loving It*, I wrote the following: "Whatever it is that you dream about with regularity, you will begin to hope for. Hope stimulates planning. Planning produces behavior designed to move you forward. This brings progress. It all begins with a dream!"

One of the secrets I have discovered for negotiating a great mate-selection deal is to find a person whose dreams are likely to take them to the very place you also want to go. Your good judgment in focusing on their dreams will make this person far more valuable than their cost.

NEGOTIATING PRINCIPLE 4:
FIND A PERSON WHO VALUES
YOUR QUALITIES

I often tell my clients that one of the most important things I have learned in my thirty-five years of clinical work can be summarized in this statement: We will always love the person most who helps us feel best about ourselves. It is crucial, then, that you select a marriage partner who makes you feel great about yourself.

When I first dated Marylyn, I immediately felt good about myself. She had such a natural way of making me feel important, desired, and valuable. This was a major part of why I was floating on air during our entire dating experience. And this phenomenon has never stopped for me.

Interestingly, the person who appreciates you so much that you begin appreciating yourself more may not be the "most expensive" person in the marketplace. What that individual has to offer you will be of enormous value, but you won't usually have to pay as dearly as you would think. And if you don't, you may end up being able to afford other features that you never could have afforded without this "price break."

NEGOTIATING PRINCIPLE 5:
LOOK FOR A PERSON WHO SPARKLES WHEN YOU'RE TOGETHER

This principle is a complement to the last one. You want to find someone who shines when you are together, someone whose best qualities soar because of your attention and encouragement. Have you noticed that some people just come alive around you, while others show little change when in your presence—maybe even acting bored and disinterested when you are together? It's just common sense that you should attend to the person whose value goes way up because of you. This can contribute greatly to your finding a magnificent bargain.

I doubt research could fully explain why some people seem to light up when they're together—while other people stay dim. For instance, I have some friends I tell jokes to, and I can count on getting a big laugh. They're not flattering me—we just have energy when we're together. Conversely, there are plenty of other people with whom my humor falls flat, and my same jokes get virtually no response. Around some people, I am cool under pressure, wise when the situation calls for wisdom, and naturally kind and generous. But others seem to bring out my less attractive sides—panic under pressure, mundane insights, aloofness, and selfishness.

If you want to negotiate a bargain, head for those persons whose qualities reach their zeniths when they are around you.

Make the "Marketplace" Work for You

Whether you like to think about it or not, the person you marry will have a set of attributes that compare favorably or unfavorably to your own. So your best chance for a great marriage lies in selecting a person within your own range—someone whose particular gifts will fulfill you at the deepest levels for the longest time.

This requires careful thought and action on your part. But you can learn to manage this part of the process so well that early in a relationship you can assess the quality of the exchange. While you definitely don't want to marry a person who will, now or in time, view you as less than a good deal, neither do you want to settle for anything other than a great deal within your range of legitimate candidates. I am convinced that you can make an excellent choice by remembering these five relatively simple principles:

First, refuse to spend a sizable proportion of your "capital" for qualities that have high but superficial value. Rather, look for "deep at the center" qualities that are likely to prove more important to your marriage.

Second, look for raw potential.

Third, find a person whose most passionate dreams for the future significantly overlap your own.

Fourth, gravitate to that person who places the highest value on your set of qualities.

Fifth, look for a person to marry who sparkles most when you're together.

If you follow these principles, you will likely end up with such a great deal that you will be celebrating your incredible wisdom for the rest of your life.

Chapter 10

How to Make an
Accurate and Early
Decision

I am supremely confident that almost everyone is capable of making an early and accurate decision about whether to continue dating a person. This is a vital decision—especially for people who don't want to waste time or risk emotional pain by sticking with dating relationships that look as if they're going nowhere. Still, some people find themselves unable to "execute" their decision—they seem incapable of expressing and carrying through on what they know they should do.

I recently talked to David Clark, my longtime handyman whom I have come to know well through the years. He inquired about my writing, and I told him the title of this book. It triggered a memory for him, and he told me a story, the kind I have often heard in my practice.

"Let me tell you what happened to me," Dave said. "I went with a woman for three years when I was younger. I knew early on that we weren't right for each other, but I really didn't know how to get out of the relationship. Every time I started to say something about going our separate ways, I couldn't continue. I was afraid I'd hurt her, or afraid that she just wouldn't be able to take it. Eventually, it went so far that we got engaged. In fact, five hundred invitations to the wedding were purchased and addressed."

"So how did you finally end it?" I asked him.

"Well," he said sheepishly, "I never did say anything, but I was acting so crazy that she eventually took responsibility for putting us out of our misery."

And then Dave went on to encourage me: "Tell people how they can communicate their decision so that it doesn't ruin the other person."

I took Dave seriously, both because of his experience and because I have met so many people who proceeded—even in the face of the "acting so crazy" danger sign. They went ahead and got married, and most of the time, the marriage was a huge disappointment—one that could easily have been prevented if one or the other person had been able to express what they knew to be a wise decision.

Six Principles for Taking Action in the Early Phases

PRINCIPLE 1: CONVINCE YOURSELF THAT THE COST OF AN UNSPOKEN DECISION WILL BECOME SIGNIFICANTLY GREATER OVER TIME

When a relationship goes on for a long time, so much bonding occurs that breaking up becomes extremely painful. As I mentioned earlier, I have seen hundreds of couples in therapy who knew they shouldn't have gotten married in the first place. But, feeling ill-equipped (or downright scared!) to talk openly about their decision, they continued on toward marriage. Then the real problems began!

For instance, I saw one couple like this in therapy, and they had four children. Now their negative decision was going to have damaging effects on four tender lives. I worked hard, as they did, to hold their relationship together, but the terrible disadvantages of their union provided an almost insurmountable set of problems. Virtually all of these "indications of mismatch" had been present in the earliest stages of their relationship. Moreover, they had identified their many differences— but then failed to act. I wonder if they might have had the courage to express their perceptions back then if they had known that their problems would never go away.

When there exist significant early problems in a dating relationship, nine times out of ten these issues will not get better. You need to become convinced of this fact. It may help you to break the bad news about a dating relationship early, when the hurt will be far more manageable.

PRINCIPLE 2: KEEP REMINDING YOURSELF THAT THE TRUTH IS ALWAYS FRIENDLIER THAN ANYTHING LESS THAN THE TRUTH

There is seldom a better time than *now* to tell someone what is true for you, especially if that truth has long-term consequences for the other person. In fact, I like to say that telling the truth to each other liberates both persons to deal effectively with that truth.

When two people begin to date, there is so much on the line. The worst outcome of all is for one person to fall madly in love with the other and not have this love experienced in return. But even this painful eventuality can be dealt with successfully in most cases—if it surfaces early on. When the truth is told, liberation begins.

You may wonder what it is about truth that is so liberating. In the case of dating and mate selection, I think it is primarily this: The ultimate goal for each person is to move toward the choice of a great marriage partner. This process, if it is to be relatively painless and ultimately satisfying, requires that the two people involved be fully informed about each other's truth during every phase of the decision-making process. When they are, they can make one small decision after another—all of them informed by the full truth—which will finally culminate in an excellent decision. But if one person hides the truth, or simply fails to tell it, the other person will likely make inaccurate assumptions and predictions. When this hidden truth finally surfaces, as truth virtually always does, all inaccurate decisions made in its absence will be painful to undo. Why is truth almost always friendlier than anything less than the truth? Because it sets both people free to make decisions that are bound to be healthy and accurate.

PRINCIPLE 3: TELLING THE TRUTH, HOWEVER DIFFICULT, CAN ALWAYS BE DIGNIFIED BY PUTTING IT INTO ITS LARGER CONTEXT

I saw a couple for therapy who were having all kinds of trouble in their marriage. Both of them were contributing to their problems but in very different ways. He was often too harsh with her, too insensitive, and what he said often hurt her deeply. In response, she would fire back in an effort to defend herself and teach him that there would be hurtful consequences when he was mean to her.

Because of the excessive anger and criticism in her family growing up, this woman was already terribly wounded and thus overly sensitive to her husband's biting comments. Her oversensitivity often initiated their negative interactions. He would bring up something just a little bit negative, and she would respond with more negativity.

My goal was to help them see what they were doing to sabotage their communication. I needed to point out their deficiencies in an effort to help them make important corrections. But my comments had to be made in such a way that I treated them with dignity. This is in summary what I said to each of them:

"John, you are unusually bright and perceptive. You often read your relationship with Jane quite accurately. But your comments make her feel unloved and put down. We need for you to put your criticisms in a form that leaves Jane feeling that you care for her, that you recognize how much she means to you, how hard you know she works, and what a vital contribution she makes to your family life. If you can do this, your accurate criticisms will get a much more positive and immediate response."

Then I spoke to the wife: "And Jane, all those times when you got wounded as a kid have made you a sensitive person. Your sensitivity plays a helpful role in so much of your life. It contributes wonderfully to your mothering, and you have a lot of friends because they value how sensitive you are. But in relation to John, I think that your sensitivity often contributes to unhelpful interactions. We need for you to 'thicken your skin' a little, erect some more effective defenses when he has something negative to say, and develop more patience toward him."

I tell you about my comments in order to demonstrate a way of putting critical or potentially hurtful truth into a context that gives dignity to another person. In my opinion, all negative truth can and should be put into this kind of dignified context.

How about breaking the bad news that a dating relationship should end? How should this be put? Let me give you an example:

"Paul, this is not easy for me to say, and perhaps it won't be easy for you to hear. But in spite of the good times we've had together, I've come to the conclusion that it's best not to continue our relationship. You're such a good guy, and I hope you know how many great qualities you have. But I am looking for a certain person who matches up well with my own unique interests and personality traits. I simply think we don't match well enough to continue dating—despite the strengths we both have. I certainly hope you can understand, because I like you very much, and I wish nothing but the best for you."

Delivering this message to any feeling person will be difficult. But think of the difference in delivering it after the second date compared to after the second *year* of dating. The truth definitely needs to be told, and the more you can embed this truth in an honest and dignified context, the easier it will be understood and received.

PRINCIPLE 4: EXPECT SOME PAIN!

If you set your mind on telling the truth only if it won't hurt the other person, you will never tell it. What we must compare, obviously, is the pain it will cause if you tell it now versus the pain it will cause if you simply wait until "a better time." If your news is negative, it cannot be told painlessly. But it's almost certain to evoke more pain if you wait until later to tell it.

Some people are frightened beyond belief at the idea of delivering painful news. They will do almost anything to avoid it. Unfortunately, they will often marry someone rather than reject them, literally lead them into a doomed marriage rather than tell them the truth that might be distressing.

I understand this, because I grew up needing to please people. I developed a terrible fear of telling any painful truth. But I had to pay for my phobia so often and so painfully that I eventually learned to face the truth, to tell it early and sensitively, to experience whatever pain was forthcoming—knowing that the long-term consequences of not telling it would be significantly worse. Most important, I learned to accept the principle that bad news can never be totally painless.

PRINCIPLE 5: VIRTUALLY EVERYBODY WANTS TO KNOW THE TRUTH

Those who would rather believe whatever is painless, even if it is not the truth, "surrender to the immediate." They choose to numb themselves now and pay in the future. Since the eventual cost of this truth-avoidance will be so much greater than simply accepting it now, most people don't let themselves fall for this fateful strategy. They want the truth—right now—even if it is not easy to handle.

I never try to tell anyone "the truth" until I am convinced it is indeed the truth. If I'm unsure of what the truth is for me, I wait to say anything. Partial truth revealed often keeps full truth from being discovered. Partial truth tends to raise anxiety for one or both persons, and the full truth thus becomes more elusive.

But once I know the truth, I deal with it promptly. Why? Because I have found that every person, at their deepest and most central place, wants very much to hear this truth. And really, they have every right to hear and know it.

PRINCIPLE 6: WHEN YOU TELL THE TRUTH, THE
RESULTS ARE ALMOST ALWAYS SURPRISINGLY POSITIVE

What a powerful belief this is! When it is applied to the communication of a negative decision about a relationship, it tends to give us the courage we need to verbalize and act upon our decision.

Sometimes it takes a while for truth to win out. I have had students and clients return to me years after the fact and thank me for having dealt truthfully with them. I have known scores of individuals who relentlessly told the truth in a dating relationship, too, and almost without exception, both parties came to appreciate the fact that truth prevailed. Not immediately, mind you, but almost always eventually.

BE DECISIVE EARLY, BUT DON'T MISS A "DIAMOND IN THE ROUGH"

At the same time that I propose new guidelines for the early detection of a dead-end relationship, I want to argue for the extreme importance of giving every relationship a chance to reveal its underlying strength. Now and then, a relationship gets started badly, but down the line, the man and woman discover they are delightfully well matched. This is the old adage about finding a diamond in the rough applied to relationships: It may not look like anything now, but polish it up and watch it sparkle!

I know a woman who is currently married to a man she initially thought was not "up to her standards." He was not as good-looking as she expected the man of her dreams to be. He didn't "show very well," and her close friends wondered why she was going with him.

But over time, as she became acquainted with his many strong qualities, qualities that were not obvious on the surface, she saw what a magnificent person he was. Although he did not have the superficial features she thought she was looking for, he was a man of such high intelligence, such impeccable character, such sensitivity that through the years she has been enormously glad that she gave this relationship a chance to evolve.

173

So the struggle becomes apparent. It is absolutely crucial to make a decision to end a relationship as early in the process as possible. But at the same time, it is equally critical to give every relationship a chance to develop and grow, if indeed it has any potential for success.

Is It a Diamond to Keep or a Rock to Toss?

Frankly, few couples terminate their relationship at an early point when it seems likely that a little patience would end up revealing a wonderful long-term partnership. But when this happens, it is clearly a serious loss, and you always hate to think that it has happened—or even *maybe* happened.

Over time, I have developed three principles to keep singles from tossing out a diamond that they thought was just a rock.

First, evaluate every person from the inside out. The qualities that really count, and the qualities that endure, are those closest to the center of a person's being. The external and superficial qualities tend to snag our attention, but the virtues that may contribute to a person's being recognized as a diamond in the rough are largely ones that reside at the center of the person—those relating to character, personality, spirituality, kindness, unselfishness, and gentleness. If you carefully evaluate these, you are likely to spot those who may "polish up" to become diamonds.

Second, if a person has none of your can't-stand qualities, but you're unsure if he or she has your must-haves, take your time! The time you are most likely to miss a diamond in the rough is when you have failed to assess a person's virtues—maybe because these virtues are hidden under less desirable external features, or maybe because they have never been exposed because of the person's shyness or unassertive style.

I know a woman who is quite shy, and she becomes anxious in every new dating relationship. She has a strong reluctance to talk about herself—and certainly a reluctance to "sell" herself. But this woman was the valedictorian of her large high school class, she is a highly trained violinist, and she is deeply spiritual. What's more, she comes alive interpersonally after several dates with the same person—she just needs time to develop trust. When she feels comfortable with someone, all of her outstanding qualities begin to emerge. Is this a diamond in the rough or not?

If you are going to find a diamond, you are going to have to be patient in the early phases of dating. So let me say it again: If she has none of your can't-stand items, but you just can't tell how many of your must-have items she has, give it time!

Third, if you encounter anyone who has a character disorder, run for the nearest exit. There simply isn't such a thing as a diamond in the rough when a character disorder is involved. (If you wonder what a character disorder is all about, review Chapter 7.) The fact is that anyone who shows signs of a character disorder or other serious emotional deficiency can never qualify as a diamond in the rough.

One of the most important struggles in finding the love of your life is to be decisive at an early point in the relationship—so that you avoid major mistakes and eventual pain while you are on the lookout for any "deep at the center" qualities that you might miss on first analysis.

Conclusion

The secret to becoming a highly efficient dater is to know precisely what you are doing—exactly who you are, exactly what you want and don't want in a marriage partner, and exactly how to read a person like a book in the earliest phases of a dating relationship. If you learn these three things, you will keep your "romantic frustration level" at a minimum, seriously reduce the amount of heartache you experience and "administer," and most likely, you will move like a rocket toward the love of your life.

I recall seeing a single woman named Jan for psychotherapy. She was thirty-two years old, moderately attractive, bright, hardworking, with a pleasant personality. She wanted more than anything to be married, but she had spent her twenties in long relationships that yielded lots of good times and nothing else. We looked closely at each of those relationships, and Jan kept saying, "I liked him a lot, but he just wasn't right for me. I knew that, but I didn't *want* to know it. I kept hoping against hope that he was the one, so I could get married and stop feeling stuck in life. I wanted to get on with having kids and building a family."

I would ask her, "So when did you know that Bob (or Jim or Bill) wasn't the right man for you?"

She would think for a moment and then make a similar comment regarding each relationship.

"Well, I guess I knew right from the beginning," she'd say. Or, "Pretty soon after we started dating, I knew we weren't a good fit."

When we had finished exploring those relationships, I asked, "So why didn't you stop dating those guys earlier if you knew you'd break up eventually anyway?"

"Because I didn't know if I'd have another chance," she replied. "I thought this might be my one big opportunity. I didn't want to give up what I *did* have and go searching for someone I feared didn't even exist."

Then Jan and I analyzed what her "hanging on" each time had cost her. It boiled down to this: For the time she was dating each of her three boyfriends, she had sent messages to every other man she encountered that she was not available. Thus, she had thrown away all other opportunities to find the love of her life while trying to make relationships work that she knew were doomed from the beginning.

SKILLS THAT WILL CHANGE YOUR DATING LIFE FOREVER

There are just three things you have to master in order to take full control of the dating process:

1. You have to get to know yourself so well that you identify precisely the kind of person you need to marry in order to be happy.

2. You need to figure out the ten most important items on your must-have list and the ten most important items on your can't-stand list.

3. You need to learn to read a person like a book—to determine if a person you date has all your must-have and can't-stand qualities.

The great news is that you can become a master of these areas. And you can learn to manage them so well that in just two dates, you will know for a fact if a particular person is worth dating. If your decision is "stop," you can terminate the relationship with dignity and respect. If your decision is "go," you can continue boldly and confidently. Either way, you are a winner.

If you have wasted a lot of time with people who don't satisfy your criteria at all, then *now* is the time to quit doing this. If you have suffered or caused too much pain because you let a relationship drag on, then *now* is the time to change. You can take control of your dating life so that you don't ever need to let a doomed relationship get beyond the second date again.

THREE PRINCIPLES TO KEEP IN MIND

First, you need to rehearse the fact that a bad marriage is a thousand times worse than no marriage at all. If you get tempted to go ahead and date someone who is obviously not right for you—all because you're afraid this may be your last chance, or because you think enough effort might turn it around—remember this principle. If you end up not getting married, it would be so much better than marrying the wrong person.

Second, the commitment you make to your own happiness is bigger and more important than getting married just to be married. In all of my seminars throughout North America, I keep stressing one fundamental truth:

You can be deeply content without being married. I'm a big believer in the magnificence of marriage, but I know thousands of single people who are profoundly content and emotionally healthy. Their contentment is much more important to their lives than marriage would be.

Third, acting decisively early in a relationship has enormous importance to your life. I've stressed this principle throughout this book, but one point has never struck me as strongly as it does now: An extremely high percentage of all marital failures are due to people refusing to terminate their relationship when they are still capable of making an objective decision. If they let themselves get bonded to each other over time—perhaps even for perfectly honorable but insufficient reasons—they will often not be able to recover their objectivity and make the hard decision that can save them from excruciating long-term pain.

You have read this entire book, and I assume you want very much to find the love of your life. I want this for you, too—very much! Let me leave you with this note of hope: I'm greatly excited about what is going to happen for you in the next year or two. There is a good chance that single people in North America are poised for the best times they have ever known. Not only do we know enough now to radically reduce the divorce rate, but there are also programs available that offer magnificent new possibilities for every single person in the world. Stay on the alert!

Here's to you and your happiness. Do what you need to do to become an expert at your own dating life. And then, may my wish for you come true: May you find total contentment in your heart—and then find the love of your life, who will be your companion, friend, and soul mate for as long as you both shall live.

ABOUT THE
AUTHOR

Neil Clark Warren is a clinical psychologist in Pasadena, California. He has worked closely with individuals and couples for more than thirty years. Dr. Warren's specialty is mate selection, and he has researched and written extensively about the complex challenge of finding, attracting, and selecting the right marriage partner. He has helped thousands of people find and marry the person of their dreams.

Included among his best-selling books are *Finding the Love of Your Life*, *Make Anger Your Ally*, *Learning to Live with the Love of Your Life*, and *Finding Contentment*. Dr. Warren's articles have appeared in numerous journals and magazines, and he has appeared on more than two thousand radio and television programs. He is a popular speaker and travels the country sharing his insights with thousands of people each year.

Dr. Warren may well be America's most widely known psychologist when it comes to matters relating to individuals who are not married but think they would like to be someday.

OTHER BOOKS AND RESOURCES BY
NEIL CLARK WARREN

Finding the Love of Your Life Program
(seven audio messages, three tests)

*Finding the Love of Your Life**

*Learning to Live with the Love of Your Life**

Make Anger Your Ally

*Finding Contentment**

God Said It, Don't Sweat It

*Also available in audio format

For further information about Dr. Warren's books, articles, and speaking schedule, please call or write:

Neil Clark Warren & Associates
300 N. Lake Avenue, Suite 1111
Pasadena, CA 91101
1-800-263-6133
www.lifelonglove.com